Dust Yourself Off, My Dear

Nine Lessons for Living Your Best Life

Dust Yourself Off, My Dear: Nine Lessons for Living Your Best Life

Published by Follow It Thru Publishing

www.heatherandrews.press
www.followitthrupublishing.com
http://www.getyouvisible.com/

Print ISBN: 978-1-5136-4983-2
eBook ISBN: 978-1-5136-5161-3

This is dedicated to all the women who self-doubt,
self-criticize and are weary. Just get up again.
You only fail when you stop trying.

Contents

Introduction

I wrote this book for the woman who is strong, but is super tired from trying to be.

Have you ever thought you would be in a different place by now? That you would be further ahead or have it all figured out by now? And well, you just *don't.* Then this book is for you.

I know what it's like to feel guilty. To feel powerless. To feel alone. I know how it feels to want to change it, but not know how to make that happen. I also know what it's like to rediscover my strength, face insurmountable challenge, and to come out the other side laughing and more powerful than ever.

Sharing what I have learned and helping others is now my life's purpose. I hope to inspire you with my story of spiritual awakening and practical change. I know you can use these nine lessons in your own life to become the person you already know you are and live the life you were meant to live. The solutions that came out of each lesson have worked for me and I know they can work for you too. At the very least maybe my tidbits of wisdom can help you avoid some mistakes along the way.

The best way to use this book is to go through the nine lessons in order because each one builds on the previous one. There are some actionable tips and suggested practices to help integrate what you have learned.

Now read the book, apply the lessons, and go co-create the life of your dreams.

All my love,

Beth

Slow & Steady Wins the Race

"Adopt the pace of nature: her secret is patience."
~ Ralph Waldo Emerson

Welcome to your first lesson. I am so excited and honored to serve as your guide through the nine life-lessons in this book. As we begin on our journey, I want to ease into it by sharing some advice that you may have heard before: slow down.

Taking time to slow down and smell the roses is not a new idea by any means, but that doesn't mean it isn't valid. Good advice never gets old. You may be wondering, "Well if it's so good, why don't more people take it?" That's a good question. The answer is that as simple as it sounds, it's much easier said than done. Especially in today's crazy world.

We live in an age where technology and modern conveniences keep us constantly on the move. It's both exhausting and distracting. If we never allow ourselves to relax, enjoy the moment and just breathe, we fall out of balance physically, emotionally and spiritually. So, slowing down really is fundamentally important to our well-being. In this lesson, I want to help you to reset, pace yourself, even start over if you wish. It is all about becoming the best version of yourself. So, let's get started.

I wish I could tell my younger self to chill the hell out. Let me introduce myself: My name is Beth, sorry Elizabeth Kathryn McMahon when I'm in trouble. Which I avoid by the way. (The Blanco is from my ex-husband and I kept it so I'd have the same last name as my kids.) I'm complicated. I'm very spiritual. I swear like a sailor (yes, especially that word). If you see, %^$# or any variation thereof just assume it's that word. I've always _tried_ to play by the rules: come to a full stop at stop signs, not drink out of the milk jug, and put a new roll of toilet paper on when it runs out. But I'm also rebellious and listen to the beat of my own drummer. If someone tells me to go left, I may just turn right instead. I had to find my own way through life, and sometimes it hasn't been fun.

My childhood was pretty normal, although who knows what "normal" is so maybe, typical of those times then. I grew up in the Midwest, the oldest of three kids to parents who got married in their early twenties. My dad worked; my mom stayed home to raise us kids. That's what most families did in the '70's. I watched Sesame Street, ate SpaghettiOs and played outside all day until it was dark. Life was less complicated then and I miss those simpler times. I didn't wear makeup until age 13 and then it was basically some lip gloss. I remember that to hear my favorite song, I had to wait for it to come on the radio. Then I would record it on a big boom box (cassette tapes- Google it to see an image) and pray the radio DJ wouldn't talk too long into it.

I wanted to grow up fast. I felt like if I got older, I would feel like I mattered more. You see I never got along with my dad. When he was home, we walked on eggshells. The atmosphere was just different and everyone felt it, especially me. Looking back now, I think he was just not ready to get married and be a dad at twenty-two, but as a kid I thought he just didn't like me. He seemed to single me out for some reason. It felt like there was always something wrong with what I did, or said or didn't do or say. My grandma (my mom's mom), who was like my angel would always make me feel special, wanted and loved. Now I know she was most likely trying to make up for my difficult relationship with my father.

The world seems to speed up with every generation. Today it moves way faster than when I grew up in the'70s and '80s. Technology is evolving at such a rate now; it is almost impossible to keep up. Don't get me wrong, there are lots of great things about our technology today. When told my kids I had to actually go to a place called a library and look through things called books to do a report for school, they were aghast. All they have to do is turn on the computer and do a search -Google, I'm such a fan.

When I was a kid, I waited all week for Saturday morning cartoons, which would air on one of only three channels that we accessed using an antenna attached to the side of the house. Now we stream. Our old TV and stereos took three strong guys to move each. Now our "devices" fit in our pockets. Everything is faster, smaller, and more available today. We communicate at lightning speed, we can get food of any kind twenty-four hours a day, and news spreads across the globe at the speed of light, travelling from its origin to our phones in seconds.

All of that instant gratification, however, has led to everyone wanting everything *right now*. There is no such thing as patience anymore.

My son Spencer, who is nineteen, seems to think that things should manifest instantly. If I have agreed to give him gas money, it should appear in his impatient little hand right now, a necessary trip to the ATM notwithstanding.

But Spencer's expectations are not exceptional. Today we all tend to want everything to happen as close to immediately as possible: we hope that a pill will make us skinny overnight, or that a work-out will transform our bodies in twenty-one days. We order a service; we want it up and running yesterday. We make a purchase online; it has to be delivered by the next day. I could go on and on.

Admittedly, patience was never my strong point even when I was a kid, so I get it. But today, there are no breaks. It is even more difficult for all of us to take time to enjoy the moment. But great things take time. A baby needs about forty weeks to develop and if it comes early there can be lots of complications. The directions on the pizza box say to leave it in the oven for 22 minutes. If you take it out at 13 minutes, it's not nearly as delicious.

I know that as a financial counselor I find myself having to explain to at least one person every week that, with money, slow and steady wins the race.

There is a reason that processes take time, you just can't rush through them. And you, my dear, are a process. So, slow down, take your time, and savor the journey. Breathe in and out, allow yourself to enjoy each stage of life, and don't wish away today. Tomorrow will be here soon enough.

What I would tell my younger self today is to relax and not be in such a hurry. I would tell her to stop wishing her life away, and being too focused on growing up, on what's next. I doubt that I would've listened anyway. The young are almost always in a hurry, it is only with experience that we learn to savor the moment.

But there is no point in wasting my time now on regrets. I lived out my youth focused on the next thing. Then, as an adult, I spent way too much time looking back as well. I spent too much time either on "shouldn't have/should have" or in "what if" or "when" mode: "I shouldn't have been in such a hurry; I should have appreciated what I had," and , "When I lose some weight, when I pay off my car, when I have $2000 in my savings account, my life will be better," "I shoulda this," "I shoulda that," "When this," "When that," I forgot to live, now!

If this is you, please stop living in those modes! They steal today. They steal your peace, your joy. There's nothing wrong with wanting to avoid the errors of the past or dreaming of the future and wanting to improve; just don't put your life on hold for either of them. Don't try to escape where you are now. Slow down and take the time to notice.

It was definitely a tough lesson for me to learn, but learn it I did. What I want you to take away is that the journey is just as important as the destination.

I chose "Slow and steady wins the race," as Life-Lesson One because before you can even decide what changes you would like to focus on, you need to slow down and get clear. You need to learn how to be present. I'm encouraging you today to relax and simply slow down. Ironically, finding inner peace, knowing how to get clear, and being able to bring some balance into your life now, will actually move you forward quicker. You will be in a better mental state for discovering what you want your life to look like. It's crazy but to speed up the changes, you need to slow down first.

If you need help with applying this lesson, check out the list below. I have put together some tips that will help you slow down and get present in different areas of your life:

1. **Create time to unplug from your technology and devices.** Technology is getting in the way of real interaction between people. Family and friends are important and people need to feel valued. According to Market Watch, adults spend up to 11 hours per day on their phones, social media, watching videos or listening to music. Relationships take time and nurturing. Put your devices away and connect with one another. Some suggestions include eating meals together as a family, scheduling a game night, planning dates to get together in person and just making time for a break from technology. When spending time with loved ones, put your phone on silent or better yet, turn it off. Give people your undivided attention and show you care.

2. **Focus on health and pay attention to your body.** There is no quick fix to your health. Whether you want to feel healthier, get fit, or lose weight, it will not happen overnight and drastic plans will only hurt you. To get generally healthier, talk to your doctor or health professional about changing your eating habits and physical activity. If you want to get fit, find out what exercise would be best for you. If you want to lose weight lose weight and get in shape, you probably need to make

changes to your diet and exercise habits. There are tons of eating plans out there, so check with your doctor to make sure that what you try is approved for you. Make simple changes. Increase your fruit and veggie intake, stop drinking pop (a.k.a. soda, I guess, in the rest of the country). It's the best change I ever made! Drink more water and get more sleep. Instead of taking food *out* of your diet, try adding more healthy choices *in*. Get 30 minutes of some type of physical activity you love at least 3 times per week. Losing about a pound per week is a good goal, especially if you want to keep it off.

3. **Taking the time for learning and growing is important**. Don't skip this part. Learning is a lifetime process that creates new pathways in the brain. It takes time, even if you are a "quick learner". I am always reading at least one book at all times, usually a self-improvement book. Some of my favorite authors are Jen Sincero, Gabby Bernstein, and Rachel Hollis.

   If reading is not your thing, listen to audio books, watch videos and movies, or take courses to expand your horizons. Take up a hobby, learn to dance, crochet, or skydive. Just don't stop growing and enriching your life.

   Consider trying meditation, which helps quiet your mind and relax your body (Just about perfect for this lesson, don't you think?). Mediation has changed my life. I began with guided meditation, where someone is either guiding you on an internal journey or feeding information to you subconsciously, such as positive affirmations. There are thousands of them on You-tube or you can download a meditation app to your smart phone.

4. **Take the time to work on your finances if this is a problem area**. Forget get rich quick. Like everything else, changing your financial situation takes time. Budgeting, paying off debt, saving for emergencies, and improving credit are all things that take time to fix. Start with looking at your income vs. your bills to determine how much is left for spending, and saving. Create an emergency fund by beginning an automatic deposit every time you get paid. It can be small, even $20 per paycheck to build the habit. I suggest making that deposit to a different bank than the one where you have your checking account so it's harder to get to. I also recommend not ordering an ATM card for this savings account. That way you have to visit during teller hours if you need to make a withdrawal. Add to it whenever you can, especially at tax refund time, if you get a bonus, or when you get those extra paychecks (twice per year if you get paid bi-weekly and four times if you get paid weekly).

When it comes to debt, consider a debt-snowball plan where when one bill gets paid off you take that money and put towards another debt. When a bill you were paying $25 towards is paid off, you add that $25 to another payment, either the lowest balance or highest interest rate account on the list. Next, pull a free credit report at either www.annualcreditrpeort.com or www.creditkarma.com and see what you need to work on. Paying credit cards down and off will automatically increase your score, but look to see if there is anything else that needs your attention. Another option for debt, especially if you have high interest cards you want to close or other debt (even if they are past due or in collections), is to use a non-profit Debt Management Program with NFCC to become debt-free. Contact them at 800-388-2227, or learn more at www.nfcc.org.

Finally, if you are not saving for retirement, start today! It's never too early to begin. If your employer has a matching plan, make sure you are maxing out their match option. If they don't have a matching plan, do something, and boost your percentage going into it every time you get a raise. You won't miss it and your retirement account will thank you!

5. **Finding your perfect career** is another area that takes time. If you love what you do, then you can skip this part but if not, pay attention. I talk to people every day who hate their jobs. If that is you, I'm not suggesting that you quit today, but take some time to reflect on what your perfect job looks and feels like. Write down in a journal all the details about this perfect job: the location, what you would do, how much you would get paid, what the hours would be, and any other criteria that are important to you. Is it a business you would love to create? Is there a side gig you could start while working your less than desirable job you have now? Do you need any training you could pursue at night while working?

   I believe in the Law of Attraction, which brings your dreams to you; however, you still need to take inspired action to open those doors. When I decided I wanted to pursue a career as a financial counselor, I started the process of studying for the exam before I even had a job. If I had not started this process, I wouldn't have even been considered. In fact, my first position was given to someone else but they decided not to relocate and I was handed the job. If an opportunity is meant for you, there will be a way for you to have it, so don't fret. Just be ready for it, and that means to take the time you need to prepare. This is also true for relationships, money, and everything else that our hearts might desire.

In conclusion, your first life-lesson is to remember to slow down, relax and take the time to smell the roses. Make the time for what is important, don't dwell on the past, and don't worry about the future. Be present and find the balance your mind, body and soul need to reset themselves, so you can begin to create the life of your dreams. Once you have reduced stress and chaos in your life, you will begin to notice the cues that your inner self is sending. Learning to trust your gut and listen to those cues is the subject of the next lesson. I can't wait to tell you all about it.

Trust Your Gut

*"Follow your instincts. That's where true wisdom manifests itself." ~ **Oprah Winfrey***

Now that you know how to slow down and take the time you need to take care of what important in your life right now, it's time to look at how you can use your new skills to get centered and learn to listen to what your gut is trying to tell you. Life-Lesson #2 is all about tuning into and following your intuition. The ego, which is defined as the part of the mind that mediates between conscious and unconscious, is responsible for handling the demands of life. It likes to keep us safe by telling us things like don't take the risk, just stay where you are because you know what to expect. Don't try. Don't leave. Don't jump. I'm going to talk about how to turn down the volume of the ego and tune into your gut, which holds the key to all the magic. And I definitely want you to experience the magic!

In my capacity of financial counselor, I always advise my clients to listen to their gut, when it comes to their finances. Especially when it's telling them that the advice their getting doesn't "feel right". I spoke to a lady this morning who was unhappy with her retirement account. She must have told me three times that it had been growing before she made changes to it. She had followed the advice of friends and her fund was now losing money. She was not happy.

I'm a certified financial counselor by trade, not an investment professional or a tax expert, but what I have is mad common-sense skills. After I explained that I don't give investment advice (my disclaimer), I suggested she follow her gut and set up her account the way it was originally, when she felt happy with it, to see what would happen. I really just listen to cues from people. It seems simple enough; If you were happy before, go back to that, right?

People don't always listen to the little voice inside. Perhaps they do not trust themselves, or aren't sure if their gut is actually their friend or just trying to steer them over a cliff. Fear is the biggest killer of dreams. What I have learned and know as truth is that your gut will not fail you. Our inner selves already know what the answer to the problem is. We just either need to tune into it or actually follow the advice we sense.

It took me years, well decades, to finally listen to my gut. As a child I was very intuitive and had a really active internal life. Back then, I had deja vu frequently, which is a French term meaning "already seen", according to dictionary.com. I'd feel nauseous, uneasy, and just weird. Deja vu can indicate a neurological issue like epilepsy; however, that was not the situation with me. I also had imaginary friends and would talk about them to my mom.

As I got older, I did my best to tune out that internal world. I was so unsure of myself that I needed to focus on what was tangible, what could be seen, touched. Now I can trace my lack of confidence to my relationship with my dad, which sucked and was filled with uncertainty, but, when I was growing up, all I knew was that I couldn't trust my gut, my feelings, my intuition. I couldn't trust anything that wasn't in front on of me; everything had to be concrete and measurable. I am also very analytical; I've always been drawn to business, accounting, and marketing classes. So, I favored my practical side and tried to focus more on left-brain stuff: numbers, facts, things I could rely on.

I threw myself into learning and spent fifteen years taking classes on and off and earning three college degrees. I have an Associates in Business, an Associates in Accounting, and a Bachelor's degree in Business. I even enrolled briefly in an MBA program for business before I realized I had enough formal education. I still carry some student loan debt from that undertaking to prove it. I went to college for years trying to make myself feel smart enough, worthy enough, good enough. Today, I would tell my younger self what the good witch told Dorothy, "You've always had the power my dear".

I began to rely on my gut instincts after I divorced. I was physically and mentally exhausted during this time and I just didn't have enough fight left in me to try to control every aspect of my life, which was my normal method of operation. I had to let go and that's when things started to change for the better. As I tuned in to my gut, I also began to develop an ability to sense, or just know, what my next step should be. This was the beginning of what I would later recognize as my spiritual awakening. It had started to blossom just as my life was falling apart.

I needed something to believe it and I needed a solid foundation for those beliefs. Something that gave me a greater purpose in life. Something that explained why I was here.

I had no formal religion at this time. My parents had gone to Catholic school and had so much of that shoved down their throats when they were kids, that as a family we only went to church on Christmas and Easter. The service was strange to me anyway, all the up down, up down stuff was not my thing. I was baptized as a baby and received my first communion at around eight years old, but that was the extent of my religious experience. Other than the occasional wedding, I don't think I saw the inside a church for almost twenty years.

While I was struggling to finish up my bachelor's degree, my daughter suddenly fell ill, and then my marriage fell apart. To say that I was stressed was an understatement. The college I was attending required a religious studies course to graduate, so I signed up and was just trying to get my credit. But something inside me stirred and I began to wake up. I wore out that poor professor with more questions than he probably had been asked before. It's rather embarrassing now, looking back.

I refer to my Higher Power as God, although I recognize that you might have another term for Him, such as the Universe or Source. Feel free to substitute the term that resonates with you.

For me, curiosity and a search for meaning turned into a hunger to know and understand God. I found a church I could attend and got my mom to come along. Then my best friend Kim bought me a Bible for Christmas that year and joined me on my spiritual journey. My world opened up so much and I felt a peace come over me that I had never in my life experienced. I began reading my Bible and learned so much that I didn't know. As a kid I had gone to vacation Bible school and knew about Noah's Ark and Adam and Eve, and of course about Jesus, but now I was learning so much more.

I found it mind-blowing that the Israelites had wandered around the desert for forty years. But then I realized that I had walked through my life for 32 years in darkness and ignorance myself.

This is when my intuition really began to reawaken. I would hear God's still quiet voice, or feel a gentle guidance in my life. I'm sure it was there all along I just wasn't listening before.

I soon grew restless in my job as a loan officer. Following my divorce, I had gone through a personal financial crisis, which took three years to turn around. I had five credit cards, a loan, and other debt to pay off. I had to move in with my mom to get through it; believe me, it doesn't feel good when a grown woman with two kids has to move in with mommy to fix her life. But, in the end, it made me stronger. I was able to get on my feet and purchase a house through Habitat for Humanity. Doors were opening up for me now, when I had always had to kick them down before.

Once I fixed my finances, I felt that I could no longer help people get into debt, which is basically what I was doing as a loan officer. I wanted to pursue something new, something more life affirming.

 I left my job of ten years to do payroll at a school system after getting my Associates in Accounting. The job was fine but the office ladies were a closed clique. They didn't let anyone else in. I left that job after about a year and went to an investing agency, which was even worse. The commute was an hour each way, the parking downtown was chaos, and I found myself in a strange new environment where I received very little training. I was miserable, literally shaking every morning as I drove there.

I pleaded with God daily for several months to help me out of there. I needed a new career; one that I loved and that set my soul on fire.

I don't know how the idea came to me, but I found that I wanted to help people get out of debt. I felt so proud of turning around my own finances and wanted others to experience that joy. Call it intuition, call it a God thing, call it a gut feeling. But I knew that was what I wanted to do.

I had no idea how to become a financial counselor or what that even meant, but I knew I had to find out. I'm not sure how, but I stumbled across my now former boss and she was kind enough to talk with me about the financial counseling industry. She pointed me in the direction of getting certified and I began meeting with clients. I didn't know exactly what I was doing, but I muddled my way through those first meetings. She kept my number and a few months later she called and said her employee was leaving and that I was welcome to submit a resume.

I applied for the position, interviewed, and received a call they had gone with another candidate. I didn't have much experience and had only completed part of the certification process, so I figured it was not meant to be. About a week later, Katherine called me back and offered me the job. Apparently, the other girl decided not to relocate after all.

The job that I was not ready for, not totally qualified for yet, and paid more than I had ever made to date, was mine. I spent the next several years learning from one of the most amazing mentors I could have ever asked for. When I came on board, she had been a financial counselor for 35 years and called herself "the oldest surviving financial counselor." Not long into that job the economy crashed; foreclosures began, unemployment was at all-time high, the bank and automotive industries needed bailing out. I had to sink or swim and do it fast. I learned more in a few short years than I had ever learned before and it made me a better counselor. I am forever grateful for that time in my life and for Katherine. Had I not followed my gut I never would have stumbled into this amazing rewarding career that I love.

I felt a strong urge to leave that job about four and a half years in. The hour commute each way was taking a toll, and my son, who was about ten, needed me. I was working ten-hour shifts, four days a week. Sometimes I would get home at 8:00 pm to find out that he hadn't eaten dinner yet, and had been running around all evening with the neighborhood kids. Our evenings were just chaotic. My daughter wasn't helpful as she didn't want to deal with her little brother and the feeling was mutual.

Again, I felt God tugging on me to make a change. I loved my job as a financial counselor however I felt that my time in that workplace was ending. The final straw was when one night on my way home, I got a call from the police. Spencer and another kid had been caught in an old school building that had been shut down for years. He just wanted to see what was inside, he told me. The cops brought him home and I don't remember if there were any juvenile charges that time (this boy has put me through the wringer). At that time, I knew I had to make a change or I would have a delinquent on my hands.

A few weeks later, I gave my two weeks' notice after the voice inside me to quit was so loud I could no longer ignore it. I did *not* have another job, I had no plan at all (which I definitely don't recommend, by the way) but once I gave my notice a sense of peace washed over me. I can't explain it but I felt pure relief even though my analytical side was totally telling me all the reasons why this was a really bad idea.

What happened next was close to miraculous. Get this, the day after I gave my notice, I got a call for a job I had never even applied for. Sometimes you have to take a step for the staircase to be built.

When it comes to my career, listening to my gut has been fairly easy. It is the area of my life where surrender has come almost naturally, I'm not exactly sure why. Maybe it's because I have always held the idea that it's just a job. I can get another one or create one. I just never really stressed about it.

I've been working since I was a senior in high school and have had a variety of jobs. I've waitressed, worked at JCPenney, and even spent eight days running a line at GM. Looking back that Temp job with GM was definitely was a God thing. It was right before Christmas and I desperately needed the money. I grossed $1500 in eight days and, although I was too exhausted to enjoy it, I got all of my bills caught up. Right after that is when I got hired at the credit union as a file clerk and worked my way into lending, which eventually led me to financial counseling. Seriously my dear, go with the flow. You'll need the training to accomplish what God has in store for you.

I got really good at trusting my gut. After leaving my first financial counseling job, I also knew I had to find another place to live. We loved our house; I had helped build it for goodness sake, but it was not in the best neighborhood. Habitat is not known for building in the greatest areas. They build where they can find lots and now have even moved into rehabbing homes for lack of land. My house was one of three cute Habitat homes with matching little sheds. They were great, all brand-new construction. The rest of the street was an eclectic mish-mash ranging from a tiny 580 sq. ft. house, to a larger bright blue construction, to one home that leaned slightly to the left. Let's just say that conditions were not ideal for maintaining one's property value.

When the recession hit and home values plummeted, my house instantly lost over half of its stated value, which had always seemed a bit questionable to me. The one thing that you can't control when you buy a house through Habitat for

Humanity is the price. The amount I was charged was more than what I should have paid in that particular neighborhood. I had to make a split decision at the closing and chose to sign the paperwork, despite being told a few months prior that the selling price would be approximately $10,000 less. My older, wiser self would have stuck up for herself and questioned the new amount but I did not have thick enough skin at that time.

Getting Spencer out of that neighborhood became my top priority. It's why I quit my job without a plan. It's why I was willing to move away from a house we had built. I started looking online for cheap houses (again, thank you Google). I had a crazy idea that I might be able to pay cash for a house while the market was in the dumps. There hadn't been a better time to buy since the Great Depression.

I took the best deal I could find and put a bid on a house out in the country for $17,000; they were asking for $18,000 (according to the sales history the sellers had paid $90,000). My bid was approved and I cashed in an investment to buy that house outright, which happened to be in the best school district I could ever have chosen and I didn't even know it yet. That move opened up so many doors for me and it literally saved my son's life. After I give you the details, you will begin following your intuition, I promise.

My new job still had that hour commute but it was part time, only three days per week. I knew I might need to pick up a second job in my area to bridge the gap, but for now, adjusting to all of the changes: new job, new house, moving, and Spencer starting a new school, was about as much as I could tolerate.

Spencer was in the sixth grade at this stage, which is a difficult time to move to a new school and make new friends -especially mid school year. He handled it like a champ, and blended right into his new life. He had always made friends easily by being the class clown; he would just make people laugh. He was also a natural athlete; I never saw his homework sheets but every time there was a sign-up for a sport, he brought it home in pristine condition.

Back in the second grade, after trying floor hockey, flag football, baseball, and basketball, he discovered his love, or maybe obsession for wrestling. One day he brought me the information for wrestling club. Wanting him to try everything and, even more, wanting to tire out his ADHD symptoms I happily signed the permission slip and we went to his first meet. He got pinned by a girl that first season. He was so pissed he wouldn't shake her coach's hand like he was supposed to. He did go apologize and shake his hand before the day was over. I thank that little girl because after that loss, the boy worked his butt off. He improved; he learned techniques. He listened to his coach's advice and a passion for the sport grew, just like he did.

His love of wrestling persisted and helped him integrate into his new school, which happened to have the best wrestling team in our county. Coincidence? I think not! God knew all along what Spencer needed and I know He led me to quit my job, buy the house, and change my life. That one thing, following my intuition to move, altered the trajectory of my life and in the most positive way that could have ever happened. Spencer has been a state champion with his wresting team *three* times and they took second place once. Individually, he took fifth place at the state tournament. Do you remember when books had pictures at the end? It may not be sexy, but I'm bringing it back. Go ahead and check out some photos of him and Marissa as well.

I have told you my story to illustrate how important it is to listen to your inner voice. My goal with this life lesson, is to encourage you to tap into your intuition more often and listen to your gut. It already has the answers and will help you stay on course. That doesn't mean you should ignore your capacity for critical thinking, it also has an important part to place in your life. The best results will come from establishing a healthy balance between your analytical and intuitive sides.

If you are having trouble hearing your inner voice or trusting your gut, here are some tips to help you get in touch with your intuition:

1. **Focus on what you would like to improve in your life.** Get a notebook and journal about what the issues are and how you would like things to be. Writing is very therapeutic and, FYI, I'm going to talk about it a lot. During a session when Spencer refused to talk to the counselor, I decided to use the time myself, especially since it was paid for. I began to unload how I was unhappy with my commute and schedule, our neighborhood, the school Spencer went to, etc. She told me I needed to figure out what I wanted my life to look

like. I began to write down all of those details. I realized that being smack in the middle of the industrial part of town was not where we needed to be. I longed for the countryside. I grew up riding bikes and climbing trees, what joy! Now there were broken down buildings for my son to explore, drug dealers across the street, and a dilapidated trailer park behind our house. To change my life, I first needed to change our environment. God tugged on me for a year. I was too scared to make the change at first, but when I finally took the leap, everything changed. The unknown is freaking terrifying but it's also where peace and joy reside. Take some time to figure out what you want and write it down.

2. **Get quiet.** You can't hear your gut if it's too noisy around you. Allow yourself to relax, get quiet and be alone with yourself. I used to pack activities in so I didn't have to spend time alone with myself. Getting to know *you* is imperative: it's how you grow. Slow down, relax, and quiet your mind. Meditation changed my life and I guarantee it will do the same for you. There are thousands of meditations of all types on You Tube. Search guided meditation and see how many choices you have or just listen to music and let your mind wander. People have this misconception that there is a right or wrong way to meditate but there's not. Some days I let my mind become still and have no specific thoughts, other times I let my mind wander where it will. There is a benefit to it all and I am so much calmer and more relaxed in all aspects of my life, thanks to meditation. It

has tamed my crazy Irish-German temper and I rarely even throw things anymore. Yes, that is a true story.

3. **Tune in on purpose and listen.** When you face a difficult decision or if something just doesn't feel right, pay attention. It may be a feeling, a knowing, or even a quiet audible whisper. Sometimes you can describe it as something gnawing at you. All of these examples are ways to describe your intuition. You can either be like an Israelite, going once more around that mountain, or you can finally give in and find the promised land. It is totally up to you but, trust me, it's less exhausting to surrender. When I finally gave up that control, I developed a peace in my life I had never experienced before.

4. **Seek out things you love to do.** Your mind and body may be craving something you have stopped doing. If you used to love to write or play music, for example, make some time for that. Women tend to give up their hobbies for their families, jobs, and all the other things pulling on them in life. It is not selfish to reconnect and find that piece of yourself again. It will actually make you a better wife, mother, daughter, sister, employee, boss.

5. **Spend some time in nature.** Connecting with the Earth, walking barefoot in the sand, or just listening to the birds can be magical. Watching the sun rise or set can take you to another place in your mind. Try going for a walk or taking your shoes off in the grass for a few minutes. Being outside is physically and emotionally grounding. It will help you improve your mood. Everything is

energy and you will raise your energetic vibration by spending a few minutes each day outside.

As you can see, trusting your gut is very powerful and can lead to dramatic changes in your life. Start paying attention to your instincts and feelings and see what happens. You may discover that people and opportunities come your way more often. It might be a new job, relationship, or situation that falls into your lap. Try practicing with in one area of your life that you want to change and have a little fun with it. Oh, and start saying yes to the opportunities that present themselves!

What Doesn't Kill You
Makes You Stronger

*"You were given this life because you are strong enough to live it." ~ **Nishan Panwar***

Now let's move on to what can be a difficult topic, engaging with adversity. We all face adversity at some point in our lives, and I think you agree that it's not comfortable or pleasant. Most of us would rather stay as far away from it as possible. Nevertheless, this lesson is all about the good that can come from the worst of situations. We'll talk about how experiences that are so difficult, so painful, will help you build up your resilience, and you'll need that strength to create the life of your dreams. The ability to use negative situations in life to drive you forward to success where others fail, is what will set you apart. What I'm talking about here is developing the ability to not only handle the stress, grief, and anxiety in the moment, but to come out of the experience stronger than ever and able to take on almost anything else that comes your way.

When I came across the quote for this chapter, I was drawn to it, at first, and then I was instantly irritated by it. My mind automatically went to "poor me" thoughts: who thought I was this strong? Why was it my burden in life to face all the challenges that had been placed in my path? Then I stopped myself.

Today, I no longer allow my mind to go there, or if it does, I don't allow it to stay long. But it wasn't always that way.

Oh, I definitely used to go there and stay there. I battled debilitating depression for over ten years. I went to work every day, but once I was home, I went to bed. I stayed in that pattern for years. I struggled to keep up with laundry and dishes. Dinner was too often from a drive-through because I didn't have the energy to cook. Many factors contributed to my depression and it didn't happen to overnight but before I get into the details and tell you how I beat it, I want to share some events that took place on September 11, 2001.

For most Americans and many other people around the world, that day was horrible. I remember it like it was yesterday. I was at work when my friend Barb announced that a plane had hit a building in New York City. The loan department at the credit union was on the second floor where our board room was. There was a television in there so we turned it on. About five minutes later we all watched in horror as the second plane hit the twin towers. My mind was racing. How could this happen in the United States of America? I was angry, worried, sad and wanted to leave, go pick up my kids, who would be turning nine and two the following month. I worked the full day, however, and picked them up at daycare as usual.

Marissa leaned her head against the car window on the way home. When I tried talk to her about the terrorist attack, she told me she had the worst headache she ever had and couldn't even talk about anything right then.

We ate dinner but she continued to complain about her head, which was very unusual. I told my mom I was going to take her to urgent care and have her checked out. After dinner she and I headed over to wait in after-hours care, which is always fun. The doctor on staff that night felt that it was a sinus infection as sometimes allergies flare up in the fall. He gave us a prescription and we were on our way. I filled it at our local Rite-aid, gave Marissa a spoonful. She said she felt awful and was going to bed. A little while later, I checked on her and she was flailing around in the bed. I had never witnessed a seizure before and this one was full-blown. Marissa was rarely sick and to say I was freaking out would be an understatement. I froze for a second but screamed for my mom. She helped me get Marissa into the car, which is very difficult when someone is jerking out of control. I can't tell you why I didn't call an ambulance; I guess I thought driving her there would be faster. She was still seizing and even knocked the gear out of drive at one point during our short drive to the Emergency Room. The details are really fuzzy but I remember yelling for help in the parking lot and this guy running over to my car to help me carry her in.

When two people carry a girl, who is seizing, into the ER, there is no waiting. Everyone jumps to attention and the doctor on duty was grabbed to come look at Marissa. I found out later that the guy who had helped me get her out of the car, had lost his best friend that night in a motorcycle accident. I had known his friend; I went to high school with him. Nine eleven had just claimed another victim.

My mom showed up at the hospital, after taking Spencer to my sister's house, and wanted to know what was going on (this was before everyone had cellphones like we do now). It was by the grace of God that the ER doctor was a neurologist. He didn't pull any punches. He told us her condition was very bad, and that she needed to be transferred to a bigger hospital- either Toledo Hospital or the University of Michigan (U of M) Hospital. I was still processing everything, but my mom spoke up saying that she knew where Toledo Hospital was, so we chose that one. Now, after working in Ann Arbor for so many years, I would probably have chosen U of M, it is recognized as one of the best health systems in the country but Toledo is also a fine hospital.

A further complication was that all flights had been grounded by the FAA due to the terrorist attacks, so we had to wait for a specialized ambulance to come pick her up.

This was over 17 years ago, so I truly don't remember all of the details, and mind you I was under the most stress I have ever endured in my life but I can tell you the highlights.

Marissa was taken to NICU in Toledo Children's Hospital where she was put into a medically induced coma. Her doctor looked me square in the eye and told me he had no idea if she would make it. Her body began curling up, called posturing, and it was not a good sign. He told me if she did wake up, she might not be the same person, know anyone, or be able to walk, talk or do any of the normal things she used to. This was my bright, hazel-eyed, curly blond girl that was eight going on eighteen. She was smart, bossy, a little spitfire and they weren't sure if she'd survive the night?

The doctors and nurses asked me so many questions. When did she get sick? Had we noticed anything going on? They kept asking about a vaccine she had received at our local health department a few weeks prior. My daycare said she needed to have the chicken pox vaccine or she could no longer attend, so I went over and got it done. As I thought back for the medical professionals, I had noticed some subtle things going on. She had mentioned the other day that she felt dizzy getting off the swings during recess; and there were a few times she seemed to be staring off into space. Neither of those things were that odd on their own, kids are sometimes clumsy and I was always daydreaming as a child. But after she was diagnosed with viral encephalitis, and I read the symptoms and signs, those were both on the list. In the end, all they could do was say that the only cause they could not rule out was the Varicella (Chicken Pox) Vaccine. The hospital refused to put that in black and white though because it is a very controversial issue. Who do you hold accountable? The manufacturer? The health department? The state? It is extremely difficult to sue over vaccine reactions unless the medical records support it 100 percent and doctors won't put it in writing. I saw several lawyers and they all told me the same thing. It's a really %#$%@ system.

Encephalitis is a brain infection, much like Meningitis, and every article I read talked about the possibility of death. For some reason, I never once thought that she would die. I was probably just naive about how serious her condition was, but this girl was rarely sick. How could she be on life support in the hospital and at death's door? It just didn't make sense.

There was another girl in the NICU on life support; she had meningitis. My sister talked to her dad while she was out smoking a cigarette and he told her she had been fine and then, two days before, suddenly she had fallen sick at school. Her whole family, including cousins, aunts, uncles, grandparents were all there. I was in the community room when I overheard them say that she was brain dead and the hospital wanted to take her off life support. The girl was fine just two days ago. I knew God could certainly take my child as well. I wasn't religious, or even spiritual, at that time in my life. I had relied on my logical brain to get me through life. It had all the answers I needed, or so I thought. But, at that moment, my knees hit the floor. I had no idea what to say, how to address the Great Almighty, but I started to plead with God. First, I apologized that He hadn't heard from me in so long, or ever. Also, that I hadn't made it to church in nineteen years, and had criticized organized religion. But then I got to the point. If He spared my daughter, *in any condition*, I promised to give my life over to

Him. I promised I would get my sorry butt to church. I probably even promised I would stop swearing (sorry about that one God). I begged with my hands together, on my knees, on the floor of the hospital with tears running down my face. I begged. I made deals. I promised that although I had no idea how yet, my life was His. And I meant every word.

Marissa Nicole Blanco was on life support for a few days before her frail body began to relax. The doctors said that although she was not out of the woods, they had some hope. She began to stir; her leg would move or her arm would twitch. The nurse said it could be involuntary and not to get too excited. I sat there and stared at her for days. I reminded God of my deal with Him and that I was counting on Him (Geez- I had been a Christian for five minutes and I was already demanding things?).

Maybe my prayers worked or maybe it wasn't her time, but that girl woke up on day five and knew who I was. The next day they kicked her out of ICU and into a regular room. A few days later, they sent her home. I wish I could say it was all smooth sailing from that day on but I can't. She had a brain injury, was left with epilepsy, and, in many ways, was a different person. She fell behind in school, had permanent medical conditions that she still deals with today (she takes thyroid medication, seizure medication, and deals with her weight). She also developed learning disabilities because of the brain damage. During the summer between her junior and senior years, she underwent a ten-hour brain surgery at the University of Michigan Hospital to remove eighty-five percent of her right temporal lobe which was all scar tissue. I wrote every one of her papers in high school so she could graduate. She couldn't even have written a simple story at that time. It took her years to heal, to catch up to her peers, and to mature. Now, at twenty-six, she is doing amazing. She bought a condo last year, is taking her pre-requisites for nursing school, and working two jobs. God is really good!

I can't honestly tell you that, given the choice, I wouldn't have done things differently. I am definitely not a doctor and my intention is not to provide medical advice of any kind here. But, knowing what I know now, I might not have had Marissa vaccinated. I could have signed a waiver, changed daycare facilities, or, lied and said she had already had the chickenpox. Not that I recommend the latter, but as a mother I would do anything to protect my child. If I had decided differently, her life would have been much easier, but then we wouldn't have become the people we are today.

We had years of doctor appointments, meeting with neurologists, endocrinologists, and a U of M surgical team who spent one of those years preparing her for brain surgery: testing, poking and prodding. She went through surgery like a trouper and was off all pain medication within two weeks. We like to joke that the hardest part of brain surgery was the hair style. She couldn't get her head wet for several weeks and she had a huge knot of matted hair that had to be cut out, which was right before her senior year began. You can imagine how frustrating it was for a teenage girl to lose a big chunk of hair, which was really hard to blend. But hair grows back and you learn not to sweat the small stuff. It was the German Philosopher Friedrich Nietzsche who said, "That which does not kill us, makes us stronger." I think back to that time in 2001 and shake my head. God must have thought we were invincible. He also thinks you are strong too by the way! I want to help you transition your thinking. Are you allowing your hardships to hold you back? Could you turn that pain and hard knocks you've faced into fuel for your greatest comeback?

Here are some suggestions for handling adversity with grace and strength and using it as fire under your ass:

1. **Feel the feelings**. Allow yourself to feel all the emotions and take time to work through them. Don't sweep them under the rug and just keep trucking on. That is a sure-fire recipe for disaster. Allowing yourself to feel sadness, anger, grief, and all the normal emotions will actually get you through the experience faster. Talk to someone, whether it be a counselor, trusted friends, or family. You can also journal out your feelings.

2. **Know you are not alone.** Take solace in knowing there is a higher purpose for your hardship. One of my favorite verses, Romans 8:28, reminds us that "…all things work together for those who love the Lord and are called according to His purposes". Even in times of despair it is comforting to think that we are not alone and that there is a larger plan working in our favor. Work on your spiritual life, whatever that means to you. Read, pray,

listen to music; do what makes you feel connected with a higher power.

3. **Practice stress reduction.** According to Healthline.com, meditation reduces cortisol levels, inflammation, and improves coping ability, among other things. Exercise a few times a week; try walking, yoga, swimming, or any fitness activity that you enjoy. Just get up and start moving, it really does release endorphins in the body, which improves your mood and general outlook on life. Rest your body and allow yourself to get good quality sleep.

4. **Get into planning mode.** Sometimes God knocks us on our butt to get our attention and wants us to course correct. Yes, it can be painful and drastic, so beware. Take this time to do some self-evaluation and see what needs changing. Journal out whatever comes up for you and get rid of any negative thoughts, feelings, or emotions. Next, write about how you wish things were in your relationships, finances, health, and more. What aspect of your life are you unhappy with? If you need to make changes, I highly recommend you get on them before God gives you assistance with it. Trust me on this one.

Life-Lesson 3 is all about developing resilience, the ability to bounce back from adversity or trauma. You can use those experiences that nearly break you in half to become tougher than you ever imagined. Difficulties, failure, or heartbreak can be the catalysts that drive you to follow your aspirations, make changes, or redefine who you want to be. Is there a dream you have put on the back burner that needs some attention? Is there something you want to start? Then get busy!

How are we doing so far? We have covered slowing down, listening to your gut, and using adversity to fuel your biggest comeback. I hope you are ready because you're about to discover just how special you are.

You Are The Prize

"Do you want to meet the love of your life?
Look in the mirror." ~ Byron Katie

This is probably the most important life lesson I have to teach you in this entire book, but you weren't ready for it until now; you had to go through the first three lessons first. Now you are ready to discover and start accepting just how special you are.

Chances are that no one is more critical or harder on yourself than *you*. Most of us would never talk to others the way we talk to ourselves. Am I right? If you struggle in this area, pay attention because understanding your true nature and learning to get off of your own back is critical if you want to live the life you were meant to live. Hold on, my dear, because we are going to dig deep into this topic.

This life lesson was the hardest for me to learn. I finally faced myself when I decided that 2018 was going to be the year that I got over my hang-ups about myself and honestly started loving and accepting all parts of me. I could not continue to evolve and up-level if I didn't feel worthy. I had thought I could skip this step, or at least fake it until I made it. But I couldn't. And neither can you. You need to get that deep inside right now.

I knew I was smart. I spent many years going after formal education to make myself feel better and I have the degrees to prove it. So that became how I valued myself, how I determined what I was worth. I can hold my own in a conversation on a wide variety of topics. I'm not half bad at *Who Wants to be a Millionaire* and there are some nights that I jam at the *Jeopardy* questions- although, truth be told, classical literature and geography are not my forte.

When it came to my career and helping clients, I had all of the confidence in the world. But, when it came to anything else, well not so much.

I know that most of my confidence issues stem from my relationship with my dad. I knew it, various counselors told me so, as did several psychic and spiritual healers. I got so sick of hearing it and continuing to feel inadequate that I finally told myself that if I was ever going to accomplish my huge dreams, I would I have to tackle this issue. It took me almost two years just to come to that realization.

I know it's hard but If you have been trying to just go around that mountain, please surrender and face it today. You can start right now, with this lesson. Hopefully my experience will push you to appreciate yourself too.

I guess I'll start with my disastrous love life. I have never had a relationship where I have felt I could relax and trust. I have always walked on egg shells, waiting for the other shoe to drop. My fears and insecurities turned me into that girl, the one who was jealous, who questioned everything, and who looked for signs that there was someone else. And usually there was. It became a self-fulfilling prophecy time and time again because my very attitude would alienate my boyfriends and push them into the arms of another woman.

I met my first love in high school; I'll call him Bobby. We were fourteen years old, which is way too young. I have bath towels older than that. It is still to this day the deepest, craziest, out of my mind feeling I ever had. Even though I no longer love him, I can remember how I felt, how insanely intense it was. I didn't want anyone else to talk to him, even look at him. I was upset practically every day about something. We were together, then broke up, then together again and continued like that, back and forth, until my senior year. When he began dating someone else and she got pregnant, I thought it would kill me, the pain was excruciating. My heart physically hurt. Finally, I had had enough and while I was getting over Bobby, I met Roger.

There were no major sparks between us but Roger was super funny, always joking and making me laugh. It was the opposite of all the pain and heartbreak I felt whenever I was around Bobby. Roger was much older also. When I was seventeen, he was twenty-two. One of the main reasons I dated him was that he could buy alcohol. I'm not proud of that now, but it really came in handy at the time. I partied a lot in high school and much of it had to do with trying to cope with my toxic relationship with Bobby. Drinking or smoking weed dulled the pain, even if it was only for a bit.

Roger and I started going together when I was seventeen and dated for five years before I became pregnant with Marissa. I was twenty-two and going to college. Even though we were together all that time, I still wasn't sure if he was the one. I had no desire to get married. At least not to him. But I wasn't miserable enough to leave either. I know

now that I was settling. If you are currently in the same place, do yourself a favor and get the hell out. Otherwise, you will lose years, and have nothing but regrets. I wasted all of my twenties. I could have gone out and found someone that set my soul on fire instead, but I probably would have messed it up. Seriously.

When Marissa was six, we broke up. He moved out but we were still back and forth. He stayed with me a few weeks around Christmas and New Year's because that's really a bad time to break up, right?

I started to feel awful and thought something was really physically wrong with me. I read about all of my symptoms on Web MD (yeah, I know medical people hate that) and went to the doctor to tell them I thought I had a cancer or some kind of fatigue syndrome. They ran some blood tests and the nurse called to say that they knew what was wrong. She told me I was pregnant. I told her she was wrong, that couldn't be. I had an IUD in, right now, this second. But she insisted that I was. My hormone level was off the charts and there was no mistaking it. She was right and Spencer Matthew is now nineteen years old to prove it. By the way, when they remove an IUD, they just grab it and rip it out. You're welcome for that tidbit.

So, I married Roger because I was not going to have a second kid and not be married; not because he was the love of my life. He married me because I said we needed to. Not a great recipe for success and I don't recommend it.

Needless to say, that marriage lasted about two years before things finally fell apart during Marissa's illness. She was in the hospital on life support and he never mentioned to any of his family his daughter was ill, much less on life support. He said he thought I was overreacting. *Overreacting?* As soon as I knew she was on the mend I filed for divorce and it became final the following April. So, I was thirty-one with two kids, one that was recovering from near-death, and trying to rebuild my life.

What I would tell my younger self, and you, my dear, is that you don't need a man to feel like you matter. I beg you to get this. You are amazing, unique, talented, and made just the way God wanted you. You do not need to change yourself, act differently, or be different for anyone. If you want to work on yourself that is great, but please don't do it to satisfy another person. *You are enough.* I say that for me just as much as for you.

In 2016, I picked up the book *The Secret* by Rhonda Byrne. The book, which talked about the Law of Attraction, had come out in 2006 so I'm not sure why I hadn't read it before other than maybe I was too caught up in the thick fog of depression. Anyway, *The Secret* changed my life and initiated my journey of self-love and acceptance.

A passage that stuck out for me was when Lisa Nichols talked about learning to love everything about herself; her mocha skin, her curly hair, her curves etc. That's when her life began to change. So, I began devouring everything I could find on the Law of Attraction. I came across something called mirror work. You look in the mirror and say nice things about yourself. "Super silly," I thought but I figured I would at least give it a try. I looked at myself and I couldn't come up with one nice thing to say to myself. Nothing. Finally, I said you have nice hair. That's it. Pretty %$#& pathetic, right? I knew I was going to have to do a lot better than that. I kept working at it, not only in the mirror but I also wrote positive things about myself in a journal every morning. Things like I'm caring, I'm loyal, I'm amazing, I have a nice smile, I want to empower others. Anything and everything I could think of, physical characteristics, personal qualities, and everything in between. I wanted to dig in and work on self-acceptance before reaching for the ultimate goal, which is self-love.

I also wanted to improve my relationship skills, so I started reading everything I could find about men and dating. You know, the Men are from Mars type of thing. I get emails and follow a bunch of relationship experts such as Rory Raye, Christian Carter, Katerina Phang, Adam LaDolce and Sami Wunder. It can get confusing because everyone has their own theory about the best strategy and sometimes, they contradict each other but I wanted to put some of the advice to practice. Once Bobby and I finally parted ways for good and I felt ready, I signed up for some online dating sites.

Tom was one of the guys that reached out to me on one of the dating sites I was on, and he seemed really fun. We exchanged numbers and ended up talking and texting for a few days. We decided to meet for dinner. The crazy thing is we knew each other. Turns out we went to high school together. Mind you I barely noticed anyone other than Bobby at the time, so Tom and I had never actually had a conversation in high school. We had a great time on our date; he hugged me and we said good night. We kept talking and getting to know each other.

I really tried to follow all of the gurus' advice: let him do the calling and texting, let him talk about himself, just listen and don't give advice (one coach says that it reminds them of a mother and will put you in the friend zone faster than anything). I don't know if it was the advice, but we were getting along really well and the more I got to know him the more I liked him. He believed in God, which is vital to me, went to church, and we shared many of the same values and beliefs.

He seemed to flake on me though, running warm and then cold; I couldn't figure out why. I didn't know it at the time but he was talking to potential employers about taking a job out of state and he was also seeing someone. I'm not sure why he sent me a message originally, other than he's a guy, but he did. We went out several times, I met two of his kids, and I even visited him in Texas shortly after he moved. We kept in touch. Meanwhile, I kept going on dates with other guys but I never met anyone else that interested me.

Recently, I traveled to Texas for a workshop and Tom and I made plans to see each other while I was there. I was really excited to see him; it had been a couple of years. You see, he is the only person that has stirred up any major feelings in me since Bobby. My plan was to tell him and see if he felt the same way.

We were having dinner at a bar and grill and drinks were involved. I am not sure how we got on the subject but he brought up the fact that he believes men are superior to women. Also, that God created Adam to rule over Eve and that she was his servant. He also proceeded to say that women should not speak in the company of men, that their role is to obey their husbands, that they should not make decisions without his permission or consent, and that they exist to take care of their man in all ways. You can imagine that this did not go over well.

Now let me first explain that I do believe that a man is the head of the household. I am traditional in the fact that I believe a man should provide for and protect his family. But what I believe a relationship should look like is an equal partnership, a team in all things including creating an income, taking care of the house, and parenting. He should be my best friend, lover, and confidant. I believe a relationship makes both partners better, it helps them grow as people. Also, this is not the 1950s where women stay home and take care of the kids and the house with a dress and pearls on. So, needless to say, the conversation wasn't well received. Actually, I wanted to punch him, you know that Irish-German temper again. I did not punch him you'll be happy to know.

The emotional fallout from that conversation has been like grieving a death. Well it was a death of something that could have been, in my mind at least. I think what I have learned is that it takes a long time to really get to know someone and not to get more emotionally invested in them than they are in you.

So now I'm back to square one, which is fine. I know my worth and I won't settle ever again. I am smart, capable, caring, and loyal. I will find a life partner that sees all that in me and more. We, as women, have to stop trying to fix these projects called men and stop investing time, energy and stress into things that are not meant to be. We need to love ourselves enough to know we deserve the absolute best, and that God will bring the right person at the right time. I believe that all of these experiences are just life lessons and until we start making different decisions, we will continue to receive the same lesson in a different wrapper. I am done trying to see the potential in a guy that is a mess. I want a man that is mature, not lugging around his baggage and will walk beside me- not ahead or behind. Rant over.

You, my dear, are the prize, and you need to remember that. You are beautiful inside and out. Your capacity to love, nurture and take care of everyone around you while you take care of your household, your children and holding it all together is remarkable. If a man ghosts you, plays games and ping pongs between you and other people, have the strength to walk away. And, yes, you may love him. Now don't get me wrong, I do believe in working on a relationship but only with another mature, stable adult who has the desire to work on it as well.

You cannot be sitting on a shelf while he's out and about with Sally and Susie and Stacie. If he has addiction problems like my ex-husband, he is not a healthy partner for you or the kids. I know it's harsh but have the strength to say, "if you get clean and sober let me know and we will see if there's anything to work on." I know it's scary. I know it's hard financially. But if you're trying to hold it together with an addict, he is sabotaging the budget anyway. While you're trying to make sure the rent gets paid, he's begging you for $20 or spending his paycheck on his next high.

Whatever his issues, you can be supportive if he is willing to work on them and get help that's needed, but you cannot, and should not, live your life through him or worse yet, give up on your dreams so you can enable his bad behavior. If you are in a toxic relationship, rip off the Band-Aid, I promise it will hurt less than if you stay, and you are worth more than that.

If you still don't know that *you are the prize*, you really need to work on increasing your sense of self-worth. Here are some suggestions for developing true self-love and acceptance:

1. **First and foremost, remember that you are the prize.** You do not have to change yourself or bend over backwards for another human. There may be areas you wish to improve; however, do it for yourself not anyone else. Make a list of your desires. What are limiting beliefs or negative thoughts that come up? Those are your triggers and things you need to work on. For example, if you would love to sing but your first thought is, I'm too this or that, work on that belief. Maybe you want to lose weight, which is fine to work on (because *you* want to, not because someone else is telling you to) but also work on reprogramming your mind. For example, tell yourself, "People of all shapes and sizes are famous singers," or "I am not defined by my size."

2. **Mirror work and journaling.** Look yourself straight in the eye and say nice things about yourself. It can be regarding physical, personality characteristics or anything as long as it's positive. Start out with a minute or two and work your way up. Do this every morning for a few weeks until you get comfortable. It will be weird the first time, but trust me it gets easier. Also start a "love yourself" journal and write positive affirmations about what makes you unique and special. Write at least 100 things, big or small. It could be as simple, such as something you are skilled at. And you don't have to write them all at once, try to add ten new items to your list each day until you reach at least 100. Feel free to keep going. Journal about your hopes and dreams too.

3. **Work on your emotional state.** You may want to talk with a counselor, read self-improvement books or articles, learn something new or expand your circle of friends. Do things you love to do. When you begin working on yourself and increasing your self-confidence you begin to shine your light everywhere. You will feel better, more confident but you also radiate from within. There is nothing more attractive than a confident woman who loves herself. If your relationship with YOU needs help commit today to focus on it. It is truly one of the biggest secrets to creating the life you desire.

4. **Learn to say "no" to things and people that are not serving you.** This was a hard one for me too. I was such a people-pleaser and I thought if I disappointed someone, they would no longer care about me. Trust me,

people that genuinely care about you will understand. It's not selfish to say no to things, it's actually self-care. If you have been working long hours all week and you agree to do something at the butt crack of dawn on Saturday morning when you should be catching up on your sleep you will resent it. You will end up mad at yourself and probably take it out on the ones you love. Do yourself a favor say no when your gut tells you to. It may be super hard and it may surprise that person at first but trust me it will be fine. You will be happy and much less stressed in the long run. You're welcome.

Learning to love yourself is vital to your journey, make sure you really integrate the principles contained in this life lesson. Self-acceptance is the key to establishing healthy boundaries. You get to decide what you will and will not tolerate in your life. When you know that you are the prize, you will expect to be treated well and will walk away if you're not. When you realize how amazing and worthy you are, the right people, jobs and opportunities will come to you. Putting yourself first will also improve your peace and joy. It will also give you the confidence to trust yourself and control your feelings in the face of adversity, which, as we will see in the next lesson, is essential for creating the life you desire.

Control Your Emotions To Find Peace

*"I cannot trust a man to control others if he
cannot control himself." ~ Robert E. Lee*

If you want to create the life you desire, learning to control your moods and emotions is an essential skill. In this life lesson, you'll learn why your feelings are responsible for everything that appears in your life, and how, by controlling them, you can achieve your goals and fulfill your dreams.

Although we all have emotions and should express them, there is a healthy way to do so. We can show anger or disappointment, but we should not let the energy or vibration of these "negative" emotions ruin our day, or, worse, destroy our life. Sometimes we just keep getting unwanted results even when we think we're doing everything right. That's when we have to dig deep and find that resilience we covered in an earlier lesson. That's when we must control our feelings so we can shift to a higher vibration and start attracting what we want instead. Believe me; I know what I am talking about. If you have struggled with your emotions, this is the lesson for you.

For most of my life, my emotions were all over the place, like the wind, and my mood followed suit. If things were going well, I was in a good mood. I hesitate to say "happy" because I was rarely happy. I did experience some good days, some joyful moments, such as when my children were born.

However, for the most part, I was just trying to keep an even keel, just trying to get through life. That is, until I realized that I was the problem.

Turns out those terminally happy people who are always so annoyingly chipper all the time, are a lot smarter than I thought. It took me decades to get it.

If you can relate to my story, I want you to know that it doesn't have to be that way. You are in control. You control your thoughts and your thoughts control your moods and emotions.

You would think that, after I gave my heart to the Lord, my life would be great. I began going to church, reading the Bible, and started to learn. But, while I had more peace in my life than before, I was still filled with anxiety and worry, and suffered from severe depression. I had the knowledge. I knew I was supposed to cast my cares on the Lord and put on the armor of God; it just didn't seem to be working for me. I prayed all the time, asking for God to fix my life and lift my burdens.

It got to the point where I kind of just accepted that this was who I was, who I was always going to be. I put a smile on my face and went through the motions. I was a pretty good mom; my kids were fed and clothed. I kept a job and paid the bills. I spent time with friends and family, made time to work out, and to even have some fun. But there was just something missing. I felt blah all the time, and always on the verge of getting upset.

I went to counseling and even tried a few different types of anti-depressants, but the side effects were as bad as the symptoms, so I quit taking them. I tried herbal supplements like St John's Wort and anything else I had read might be helpful. I've always believed in natural remedies and allowing the body to heal itself but, unfortunately, they didn't work either.

I did feel a lot better after we moved to the country where we still live today. I loved the quiet and serenity of living in a don't-blink-or-you'll-miss-it town. We have a big yard, corn fields around us, and privacy. I thought that when we moved here, I would just snap out of the fog, but it didn't work out that way. I lived in that a state of, "I'll feel happy when…" that I talked about in the first lesson: when I find that perfect job, when my kids are grown, when I meet the love of my life. When, when, when. I was wishing my life away, again, just like when I was a kid. I think that I probably wished away half of my life, overall.

I remember that my mom would always say, "Fake it until you make it" and it really irritated me. I would tell her that she had no idea how I felt. But the truth was that she had a "glass half full" mindset that I envied. She has always had a relatively optimistic outlook, even though her childhood was far from perfect. She could easily have opted for pessimism instead. I, on the other hand, had not come to terms with my childhood issues, and, as I discovered, that was what was holding me back.

Like most people, when I was growing up, life had its ups and downs. Family members, dealt with their demons in their own way. My grandma, for example, had issues with pills and alcohol. I remember one time, when I was a child, we got to her house and she wouldn't open the door. My mom could hear her in there and knew something was wrong. She got the neighbor and they broke in the door. We found my grandma in her recliner with the metal part that holds up the leg rest all the way through her foot.

Witnessing an event like that, probably affected me on some level; it certainly left an impression. But I think that most of my emotional baggage came from my relationship with my father, who had issues of his own.

I felt like he never wanted me around. He was always yelling and mad about every little thing. He worked a lot and did side jobs on the weekend. He was very mechanically inclined and could fix or build anything- a trait I did not inherit, unfortunately. He learned pipe-fitting welding in the Navy and became a maintenance supervisor, fixing and maintaining all of the equipment at chemical companies. He also spent a lot of time in the bar and was on several pool leagues. I felt much better when he wasn't around, especially if he had been drinking.

Over the years he and I have definitely had our problems. In my junior or senior year, he showed up one time and signed me out of school. He needed to talk because his current girlfriend had broken up with him. We went to lunch and then he brought me back to school. It was one of the only times that ever I remember feeling needed or important to him. My mom, however, was less than thrilled when I told her about my adventure that day.

Eventually, my dad got his life back on track and got married for a second time. My step-mom was awesome and really did her best to make my sister, brother, and me feel included. She was good for my dad, helped him rebuild his financial life and, eventually, they were able to buy a house. It seemed he never could stand for things to go well for too long, though. A few weeks before my wedding, they were separating and getting a divorce. After that, my relationship with my father got pretty rocky again and really never recovered. He got married for the third time a few years later, to someone he had apparently dated in high school. I haven't talked to my dad in over ten years now. I reached out when Marissa turned sixteen and tried to invite him to her birthday party. I was told to %$#& off, so we will probably never speak again. His loss.

I am surprised at how easily I can write down those words now. Those thoughts used to send me into a downward spiral. I mean, what kind of person must I be if my own father doesn't talk to me? I have made peace with it and done lots of inner work and healing around it, but at the time that the main story in this lesson was taking place, after we moved to the country, I had yet to come to terms with my relationship with my dad. I was doing all of the "right things" but I still felt like crap; I had no control over my emotions, and my moods continued to be erratic. But come to terms with it, I did, and this is how.

I told you about the impact that *The Secret* had on my life. It talked about how we can achieve anything our hearts desire: money, health, relationships, happiness. And it said that we all have the power within us already. The Law of Attraction, which is a universal law like gravity, says that, if we know how, we can use our thoughts and emotions to fulfill all of our desires and realize all of our dreams. The key is to remember that like attracts like! Positive emotions attract positive outcomes, while negative emotions attract negative outcomes. You see how it works?

Learning about the Law of Attraction lit my soul on fire and I felt that I had finally found the piece that was missing in my life. Just to clarify, it did not replace my faith or beliefs in any way, just enhanced them. The Law of Attraction exists, *in addition to,* not *instead of.* I immediately started devouring anything I could find on the Law of Attraction. Two of my favorites are anything by Abraham-Hicks and *The Universe Has Your Back* by Gabrielle Bernstein, although there are literally thousands of books, videos and articles out there on this subject.

It all made so much sense to me now! It didn't matter if I was *doing* the right things; inside I was always upset, anxious, and depressed. How could I expect for good or even great things to show up in my life?

I remember that one year, within a few months, I had a speeding ticket, a fender bender accident, and, while I was driving down the road on the highway, a tire blew off the back of a truck right in front of me. I had no choice but to run over the tire, as I was going 70 mph and could not avoid it. It ripped the oil pan off the bottom of my car and destroyed the transmission. Afterward, I got letters from the State of Michigan that said that because I had accumulated so many points on my license, I had to pay a driver's responsibility fee *and,* if anything else happened, I would have to attend traffic school! None of it was my fault and I was fuming.

I can tell you that ever since I began applying the principles of the Law of Attraction, I've had an excellent driving record and I no longer I have any points on my license. We really do attract both positive and negative things into our lives.

After *The Secret,* my life began to change. I finally knew what I needed to do. I decided I was only going to attract positive people, experiences, and situations into my life from now on. Once I understood that as long as I allowed depression and anxiety to have a grip on me, nothing in my life would improve, ever, it was like a light switch. I may sound overly simplistic, but I just decided that I was going to be happy and look for opportunities to laugh and be joyful. I guess my mom's advice of "fake it until you make it" was right all along (darn it!).

I began to smile more, and to do things that I enjoyed doing. I stopped watching the news because it always seemed to bring me down. I became more positive and began saying hello to strangers. I thanked the girl at the drive through and told her to have a good day, I waived at the dancing Statue of Liberty in front of the crazy tax prep place. I stopped waiting for "when" to be happy and decided to feel happy now.

You can let something ruin your day or you can shake it off and move on. I now choose to let stuff go and I encourage you to do the same.

Practice positivity in your everyday life. Get intentional with it. Find reasons to smile and look for ways to acknowledge others and to lift up your own spirits. Avoid any kind of negative speech. Quit saying things like, "I have the worst luck," "I'll never make it," "I can't afford it." I want you to flip your thoughts and begin to think that you *will* accomplish your goals, that money *is* coming your way, and that you not only have great luck but you attract positive things in your life. Wouldn't it be amazing to stop chasing everything you want and have some things come looking for you?

Trust me, it will take some time to break your old habits. Although everyone will proceed at their own pace, this is one of those processes that takes whatever time it needs to resolve. As we discussed in the first lesson, some processes don't have shortcuts and you can't speed them up. You'll have hiccups along the way, you'll take two steps forward and one step back a few times, but keep going.

It has been over two and a half years now since I discovered the power of positivity and I have changed so much. I still feel down now and then; I just no longer stay there and I don't let it overwhelm me like I used to. I will do whatever it takes to change my mood, such as listen to music I love, get up and dance, pick up a positive book, or check out a Tony Robbins video on You Tube. I love listening to Oprah, Joyce Meyer, Abraham-Hicks, and Eric Ho. I also try to get to the gym a few times a week and I work out with a personal trainer who pushes me beyond my comfort zone.

My dog is my bff and brings me immense joy. His name is Yolo, which is what happens when you let a thirteen-year-old name a dog. I just realized that that makes Yolo six years old now, which is about half the lifespan of a Springer-Lab mix. I plan to revel in every precious year with my pooch. Find whatever brings you joy and go after it. You don't have to spend a lot of money, taking a walk or watching an inspirational video on You Tube, is free.

Let me be clear. I chose to use the Law of Attraction to help me get past my depression and other issues that were interfering with my ability to lead a happy life. I have had a lot of success with it, but I am not suggesting that you should forgo traditional counseling or stop taking any prescribed medication. I am just letting you know that if you have tried that route and are still struggling, there may be another answer.

Initially I tried therapeutic options, prayed to God, did everything I could think of to improve my life, but to no avail. Ultimately, I accepted my fate. I assumed that my family history of depression explained my own and that it all came down to genes. If you identify with my solution, if you are having a similar experience, then consider using of the Law of Attraction to improve life and make an effort to think more positive thoughts on a regular basis. See what happens. What do you have to lose?

I hope that some of you are experiencing some aha moments right now like I did. When you realize that you carry with you the power to change your life any time you want, it's like turning on a light switch; it's incredible. And, the beauty of the Law of Attraction is that it is so simple. Just remember that it all begins with your thoughts and feelings. Make the conscious decision to *feel* good, happy, and joyful on purpose, to activate dramatic changes in your life and to, finally, get a handle on your thoughts and see-sawing emotions.

If you're not sure where to start, look no further than the list below. You'll find my best tips for controlling your moods and emotions, and getting the Law of Attraction to work in your favor. They helped me overcome depression, anxiety, and to finally find peace; I know they can help you too.

1. **Make a list of what brings you joy and makes you smile**. Start doing more of that. And also avoid what makes you upset or brings you down. I had to stop watching the news or reading anything negative. Sometimes my mom or daughter will tell me if something important happens and I need to know about it. I don't live under a rock; I do catch some news on Facebook or online and it seems to go over better from those sources. I avoid scary movies because I don't like violence of any kind. You'll discover for yourself what you can and can't tolerate and adjust accordingly.

2. **Create a dream journal.** Make a detailed list of what you want out of life. Use all of your senses: sight, smell, taste, touch, and sound. For example, if you are writing about a new car talk about the new car or leather smell, how the stereo system or engine would sound, how the steering wheel would feel and include all of the emotions around the whole experience. Find a photo of a car you would love to have and paste in on a board. Visualizing is very powerful.

3. **Stop yourself if you get upset.** Learn to recognize your triggers. Try to avoid them, if possible, or find new, healthier ways to cope. Let's say your ex knows how to push your buttons, just stop allowing it. Respond differently or not at all if you can avoid it. Traffic is still an area I struggle with, and I have to catch myself getting upset. I will do some deep breathing, or turn up the radio, so I can shift my focus. It may be difficult at first because behavioral patterns develop over a life time but I promise it will get easier if you keep at it.

4. **Meditation.** Yes again. I say again, meditation has genuinely changed my life. I knew my depression stemmed from my childhood so one of the first meditations I practiced, after I started getting serious about it, was for healing my inner child. It was a really powerful experience that I definitely recommend. You go to You Tube or download a meditation app to your smart phone like *Calm* but, whatever you do, I highly recommend that you make meditation part of your daily routine. It is probably the single most effective solution I

have found to help me relax, and I have dealt with anxiety for most of my life.

5. **Be positive on purpose**. Smile at strangers or say hi, whether they respond or not. Say thank you when dealing with anyone in the service industry: ordering food, picking up your dry cleaning, or buying groceries. And tell them to have a nice day while you're at it. Brighten someone's day intentionally! If people just started being nice to each other, can you imagine what the chain reaction would be?

6. **Try to laugh every day.** Watch a funny movie or a video that always cracks you up. I love the late Robin Williams. That was a huge loss. Thankfully he can still make us laugh, just google, "Robin Williams explains the game of golf". I'm giggling right now just thinking of it. Listen to any comedian that makes you laugh or watch a show you find hilarious. I read a quote recently that one minute of anger weakens the immune system for four to five hours, but one minute of laughter boosts the immune system for *24 hours*.

7. **Be willing to tackle the underlying issues.** In my case, I knew that it was all about my daddy issues. I had to get to the point that I was willing to face the pain so I could be free forever. If you're feeling brave, journal about it. Write down anything you want or wish you could say. Don't worry, you will destroy the pages when you are done so don't hold back. You could write a letter to someone or just vent about anything you want to get out.

You may have to do this several times. There's layers, baby, and you will need to work hard to peel them all back. I have done this multiple times and each time I have dug deeper. When you are finished shred it, rip it up, or even burn the pages. Try journaling during a full moon, the energy is wonderful and it is a great time for releasing those emotions.

8. **Try Emotional Freedom Technique (EFT) Tapping.** EFT is a practice that involves tapping on specific points on your face and body in a specific way to reduce anxiety and stress. It is a very powerful technique that can help you work through minor to severe emotional issues. Go to You Tube and search for "Tapping Videos", you'll see what I mean.

9. **Find your purpose.** Many times, depression takes over because we feel unfulfilled and lacking in a purpose. Take your focus off yourself to help others or create a project that lights you up.

10. **Get rest and proper nutrition.** Our body cannot ward off depression and anxiety if we are not feeding it well or getting enough sleep. Try drinking plenty of water with a little lemon juice. Have some first thing in the morning. It is naturally alkalizing for the body. Keep your food as natural as you can, cutting out as many processed foods and artificial sweeteners and flavors as possible.

Now you know why it is so important for you to learn to control your moods and emotions. It is critical if you want to take charge of your life and create the future you desire.

The conscious use of the Law of Attraction will be one of the most powerful tools you will ever use to change your life. If you struggle with your temper, depression, and anxiety, I completely get it because I have been there. I know how hard it can be. Controlling my emotional state has been the biggest deliberate change that I have made to improve my life. Working on my attitude, emotions, and mood has completely transformed my life. I you choose to follow this path, you will discover new levels of happiness, joy, and peace that will affect all areas of your life. Remember that like attracts like, so get positive now, in preparation for the next lesson!

Forgiveness & Gratitude Are The Biggest Secrets For Success

"When I started counting my blessings, my whole life turned around." ~ **Willie Nelson**

In the last chapter you learned how important a positive mindset is for creating the life you desire. Now, building on that lesson, we are going to explore two practices that will increase your ability to stay positive and help you achieve more happiness and contentment than you ever thought was possible: forgiveness and gratitude. We're covering them together because when you practice both, they intersect on the emotional level. If you feel truly grateful for everything in your life, forgiveness is easy; and when you forgive, you make room in your heart for gratitude and love.

First things first, let's define our terms. *Forgiveness* is defined by Wikipedia as the "intentional and voluntary process by which a victim undergoes a change in feelings and attitude regarding an offense". Even the definition is heavy stuff! Basically, my intention regarding forgiveness is to help you free yourself from anger, guilt, and old grudges so you can live the life you were made to live, without a huge chip on your shoulder. *Gratitude* is appreciation and being thankful for what you have. It is the secret sauce that keeps the blessings flowing into your life. Now, hold on, my dear, and take some notes. It's going to be a wild ride.

Let's start with forgiveness. It's good for your health and good for your soul: according to the Mayo Clinic, some of the health benefits are lower blood pressure, fewer symptoms of depression, improved heart health, and a stronger immune system, to name a few. And, under the principles of the Law of Attraction, *lack* of forgiveness holds us back from becoming all that we are meant to be. It blocks blessings from coming into our lives.

So to summarize, forgiving makes you healthier and happier and *not* forgiving can leave stuck and prevent you from thriving. Sounds like forgiveness is a pretty good thing. So why don't we do it more often?

Forgiveness is mentioned well over 100 times in the Bible. In Matthew 18:21-22, when Peter asks Jesus how many times he needs to forgive, Jesus answers, "Seventy times seven", which means over and over again. I believe this is because forgiving someone is not easy. I am not sure why, but I think it might be because forgiveness is often confused with weakness. It also gives us a reason for the anger we are carrying. Whatever the reason, most human beings would prefer to hold on to a grudge.

I should know because, for most of my life, I was really good at holding grudges. So much so that, even after the spiritual awakening that followed Marissa's illness, I was still not ready to fully embrace forgiveness. I was reading the Bible, but I was still picking and choosing what to incorporate into my life and what to leave out.

When I finally decided to start practicing forgiveness, I knew I was harboring ill feelings toward many people. Yep. I had a lot of grudges. And, those were just the ones I could name off the top of my head. There were probably many more under the surface. Boy, that was some chip I was carrying around on my shoulders. No wonder I was dragging.

I started with the obvious: my dad and Bobby. I journaled more times than I can count. I wrote them letters (that I destroyed afterward). I did journal dumping, which is writing down anything and everything that comes to mind and continue to write until you run out of things to write. I did releasing during the full moon, where you write what you want to get rid of the evening of a full moon and then destroy the page. I also did healing meditations and cord cutting journeys, which helps you to release negative connections (you can find some examples on YouTube).

Forgiveness really is necessary if you want to be free from the pain of your past. By the way, you do it for *you*, not the other person; you are the one being held in chains. The other party is out enjoying life. They probably aren't thinking about you and they certainly aren't worried about how they have wronged you. Meanwhile, you are stressed out, upset, and not fulfilling your purpose. So, let it go. I promise you; it will be so worth it.

My dad and step-mom completely stopped talking to me over ten years ago. One of the issues was that my step-mom didn't want to be around my mom. My parents had been divorced for over 20 years, mind you, when my dad married his third wife, and she had no reason to feel threatened by my mom who no longer held any interest in him. It became difficult whenever there was a family event like my college graduation or my kids' birthdays. I was not going to exclude my mom. Finally, they just stopped speaking to me. I wish I could say it was fine and it didn't even hurt anyway, but that would be a lie. Rejection always hurts.

I was angry and held a grudge for years. I have only seen my dad once since our last conversation on the phone. It was at my aunt's funeral and I did not speak to him. Spencer, who was eleven at the time, went up to him and scolded him for not talking to me; it didn't do any good.

One time, Marissa saw him at the local hospital when she went to visit her friend who had just had a baby. He didn't recognize her, which was a relief to her. It is kind of strange knowing you have a parent walking around within thirty miles of where you live and you don't talk to them. I stuffed the feelings down for a long time and tried not to let them surface.

When I started studying the Law of Attraction, forgiveness was a constant theme. Geez, it was so annoying. But, as I worked on developing a more positive mindset and learned to control my feelings, it became clear to me that I would have to confront my issues around forgiveness eventually, if I wanted to take my life to the next level. That didn't make it any easier. And it's not easy.

I have written whole notebooks of journal entries on forgiving my dad. I have worked for over two years on this topic alone. Just when I think I have completely healed, I get triggered, which lets me know that I'm not there yet. So, I work at it a little more. I've made a lot of progress though. I would never have believed I could type these words for all the world to see. Especially the part about my dad. It has always been a touchy subject. I used to clam up; I couldn't talk about it. Now I feel free enough to write this book and I even started a Facebook group called Healing From Your Childhood to help others heal and be set free.

Now, let's move on to Gratitude, the other powerful practice that is the subject of this lesson. The more you practice gratitude, the freer and lighter you will feel. Not only will forgiveness come more easily, everything in your life will flow more smoothly. Being thankful really helps bring even more blessings into your life.

According to happify.com, people that practice gratitude experience more happiness, feel more alive, express more kindness for others, sleep better, and even have improved immune systems. So like forgiveness, gratitude not only feels good, it makes you healthier.

If you can appreciate anything small or large that comes your way, you will be given even more. I'm talking about the most minor things. If I get a good parking spot at the store, I say thank you. If I find a quarter on the ground, I am grateful and express it. I encourage you to start thanking

God, the Universe, whatever term you prefer, today, and watch the blessings start raining down on you.

Another trick is to appreciate what you already have, even if it is not your ultimate desire. For example, have gratitude for your old car with 150,000 miles on it. If it gets you back and forth to work and starts up every time, that is a blessing. Maybe you want to upgrade to a cute little Jeep; be grateful for the one you have and the car of your dreams will more likely to come your way.

This chapter is short but that doesn't mean it's not important. Quite the opposite, actually. Both Forgiveness and gratitude are necessary for achieving true self-realization. You can work on both or take them one at a time.

You can start working on forgiveness today. Don't deprive yourself of your best life. Once you begin to forgive, being thankful is just the natural next step and it's easy, once you have shed those old grudges and all of that bottled up anger.

Conversely, if you are really struggling with forgiveness, try making gratitude a habit first. When you start feeling lighter and happier, you will lose those feelings of resentment and your ego won't control you as much. That's when you'll be able to tackle forgiveness again.

Here are some ideas for working on forgiveness and gratitude:

1. **Make a list of everyone you can think of that you are angry with.** Write each one of them a letter with anything and everything you would love to get off your

chest. Don't worry, you are not going to send it, so get it all out. When you are done, destroy the letters: rip them up, shred, or even burn them.

2. **Talk to someone.** It could be a counselor or just a friend but talking things out is healing. You may just need to get it out or that other person may have a perspective that could be helpful. Either way, don't hold things in. The only way to deal with anger and grudges is to face your emotions.

3. **Meditate**. Yes, this again. You'll find that meditation has many applications and is helpful for both forgiveness and gratitude. You find many relevant meditations on You Tube. Check them out or just listen to music and reflect on forgiving someone or appreciating something.

4. **Work on saying thank you several times per day.** Start with when: you get a green light in traffic, you find a good parking spot, you get the elevator right away, or the kids get ready in the morning without a fight. Anyway, you get the idea. Just begin saying thank you, either in your head or out loud. As more and more positive occurrences begin to appear in your life, don't let up. Keep expressing gratitude.

5. **Start a gratitude journal to keep track of all the things you are grateful for.** Or, you could make a gratitude jar and put in slips of paper with the things you are grateful for. Add a few each day. Decorate the jar; make it fun. Another project you could do is create a gratitude wheel. Put the words "Thank You" in the middle and create a

wheel (similar to the Wheel of Fortune wheel) and put items you are grateful for around it. Make it colorful and go crazy.

In this lesson you have learned about two new powerful practices that you can use not only to free your heart and mind, but to maintain and reinforce a positive mindset. When you learn to fully engage with forgiveness and gratitude, you will be so full of positive energy that the Universe will have no other choice but to send you but good things. Now, you're ready to move on to surrender. That's going to be a heck of a life lesson. See you there!

You Are Not In Control

*"You must learn to let go. Release the stress. You were never in control anyway." ~ **Steve Maraboli***

One of the best ways to reduce stress in our lives is to start giving our problems to God (Spirit, Universe, Source). It is a form of surrender, a surrender that feels like a gain not a loss; that is, once you are willing to take the leap. Again, this stuff is simple but not always easy.

Surrender was also very difficult for me. Relinquishing control doesn't mean we're weak or not capable, it just means it's not our job to oversee it all. This is a very is valuable life lesson to learn because if you relax a bit and just *allow*, you will be pretty amazed at the results. However, if you try to control everything, it will just end up being a big shit show instead.

I used to try to control everything (well other than my moods, thoughts, or emotions!). I tried to control people, situations, and outcomes; in other words, precisely what we can't control. It didn't work; I was miserable. But, when I actually started to let go, to surrender, I felt so much peace.

It was much easier to go about my day knowing that someone else is steering the ship. My absolute favorite Bible verse is Jeremiah 29:11: "For I know the plans I have for you declares the Lord. Plans to prosper you and not harm you. Plans to give you hope and a future." That quote still gives me goosebumps. When you *know* deep down in your soul, that someone loves you and has a plan for you, not just any plan but *great plans,* it blows your mind.

It takes some practice, but try to relinquish control and see what happens. If you are a strong-willed person, it will be difficult but it will also be a relief when you realize that you can relax a bit.

Earlier, I shared with you that I've been handed jobs when I needed them, including one I hadn't even applied for that just came looking for me. I was also provided with a house in the best possible school district for Spencer. I know that I was not in control of those situations; my role was limited to recognizing the opportunities I was given and following my instinct to act. Had I not searched for houses, for example, our move wouldn't have been set in motion.

But just because you think you are doing everything the "right" way doesn't mean that everything is always sunshine and rainbows. Why does God allow bad things to happen to good people? Why do children get cancer or born into places without clean drinking water or enough food? I can't answer that. We are the hands and the feet. Maybe we are meant to come together as human beings so we can solve these problems together. Maybe that's the plan.

I was diagnosed with Juvenile Rheumatoid Arthritis at age two and have always dealt with problems in my right knee. My doctors have assured me that I will need a knee replacement at some point - that's a *when,* not an *if* type of scenario. Initially, I asked, "why me?" But I have come to accept it.

Remember, when we talked about adversity and how it should be treated it as a life lesson? Well, sometimes the life lesson is hard to spot.

On Thanksgiving Day, when Marissa was driving to work, a truck pulled right out in front of her. She tried to swerve to miss it and ended up hitting a tree in someone's front yard. The car behind her plowed into the truck. Rescuers had to use the Jaws of Life to get her out and she still remembers nothing until the moment the paramedics were putting her in the ambulance.

When I went to clean out her car at the salvage yard, the car was crushed like a tin can. It was a miracle she had again escaped death. We joke that she must be part cat and I thank God for her feline qualities.

Although, she did have to use a walker for a few days, nothing was broken and the whiplash and bruises would heal. She just finished up her last week of physical therapy as I type these words, and she is doing really well.

It is a little hard to see what we were supposed to learn from the accident. Maybe it happened to prove again how resilient she is. But we already knew that. I know there is a reason for everything that happens, but sometimes it is hard to figure out Maybe understanding will come later.

Other times the life lesson is all too clear.

If you are not listening to the small, still voice, God will keep speaking anyway. He is like a GPS, continuing to recalculate if you go the wrong way. It may add years to your trip, but you'll eventually get there. Isn't it great to know that?

If you ignore the whisper too long, though, He can, and will, pull the rug out from under you. You can believe it won't be pleasant.

Spencer is drawn to friends who don't always use their best judgment. He has a hat that says "Bad choices, great memories", which sums Spencer up in four words. There was one particular kid he hung around with that was honestly just bad news. I warned him, his coach told him, and so did others, but he wouldn't listen. Their friendship had seemed to cool though, so I was surprised to find this kid at my house one morning this past summer. I had gotten up and found him in the dining room. I asked him where Spencer was and he told me he was sleeping. I planned to have a stern conversation with my son when he woke up; he knew I didn't want that kid over. But it was 5:30 a.m., so I went back to sleep.

I got up again around 7:00 a.m. and took my dog out. I noticed that the car Spencer drove was gone. It was fourteen years old, handed down to my daughter first and then to Spencer, but it drove like a tank. I tried to wake Spencer up for several minutes, asking him where his car was. He finally woke up and said he had no idea about the car and he didn't give his friend permission to take it. By then, I was fuming!

Spencer called and sent his friend a text but, received no answer. I was about to call the police to report my car stolen when *they* called me. The car had been in an accident and I needed to get to the scene. I made Spencer get up so he could drive the car home.

The problem was that the car was totaled and wouldn't be driven anywhere again. What transpired next, would change the course of Spencer's life forever.

His friend, who wasn't even a licensed driver, had a bag of weed on him and was in the back of the police car. Spencer was on probation for a fight he and I had gotten into the summer before. Had he completed all of his court requirements it would have been a different story but, since he had not, his time got extended. A person on probation is not supposed to hang out with people that possess drugs. That was problem number one. He was taken to report to his probation officer who made him give a urine sample on the spot. You can guess what happened next: he tested positive, which was a violation. Big problem number two.

Spencer ended up spending half of the summer between his junior and senior year in the county jail. That was bad enough, but the chain of events that was set into motion is heart wrenching. The athletic director was given a copy of the police report and Spencer was cut from the wrestling team. Spencer's only passion in life had just been stripped from him. He was a back-to-back state champion with his team and ranked 5th in the State of Michigan individually. He would not be allowed to wrestle during his senior year of high school. That last sentence was harder to type out than anything I've said about my dad. It's still so raw; wrestling is in mid-season right now.

That will be one life lesson that will be etched in Spencer's memory forever. I wish I could say he was good with it and life has been smooth. It hasn't. Spencer was suicidal and I thought I was going to have him checked into a psych ward. He lost his relationship with his coach, who was like a father to him; and most of his teammates. He was a changed person. He switched to online classes because he could not bear to go to school and see teachers and friends, especially any of the wrestlers. He has been a wrestler since 2nd grade; it's who he is to his core. When he wasn't practicing, or wrestling, he was watching wrestling videos. I videoed all of his matches and I would hear him in his room watching them. This kid lived and breathed wrestling; now he'd lost his oxygen.

I know you could say he did it to himself. He shouldn't have been hanging out with this kid; he shouldn't have been partying, especially since he was on probation. I agree with all of that but losing wrestling in his last year of high school was really harsh. If he hadn't been very good at it or hadn't loved it with every part of his soul I wouldn't feel so badly. But, then again, it wouldn't be a life lesson, I guess.

Lessons tend to hurt and this one cut to the quick. Not just for Spencer but for me too. I had really wanted to see what he could accomplish in his senior year. Now I feel like it's unfinished. If you have ever seen high school kids march around in a huge arena to "We Are The Champions" by Queen, then you know how I feel. I know it will get easier and he will always have tons of amazing memories to look back on.

What I want you to take away from this lesson is that there is a plan for you, too. You can ignore it, get off course, take off in the opposite direction if you choose, however, God has a way of turning us around. It's not always in a cute "here honey, come this way" kind of manner either. He will rip people out of your life, knock you on your butt, or leave you in the wilderness wandering around, if that's what it takes. If you need to hit rock bottom so you realize the only way is up, that can be arranged as well. So, what I suggest is, if there is something you know you need to change, get working on it today.

When we refuse to let go, we are saying we do not trust that there is a plan in the works for our highest good. Trusting is not always the easiest thing to do, but I promise it does get easier. Even when your life seems to be in a total mess, that just might be when it's about to turn around.

The following list are my suggestions for helping you surrender and let go:

1. **Focus on what you can control.** The things to work on controlling are your moods, thoughts and emotions. Work on being positive on purpose and not allowing negative moods to worm their way in and stay. Journal out negative thoughts and beliefs. Get rid of them. Finally, make sure you are tuning into your intuition; it is a wonderful guide.

2. **Visualize.** Meditation and visualization are super powerful techniques to help you relax and let go of control. Focusing on how we want things to be can release our attachment to how we get there. We don't have to know every detail to be satisfied that things are falling into place. Meditation has so many benefits: reducing stress and anxiety is right at the top of the list.

It is also excellent for accessing our intuition and taking cues from the Universe.

3. **Manage your health.** Your health is important. Focus on eating well, getting plenty of sleep, engaging in physical activity, and drinking lots of water. There is a lot about your health that you can control, so take the time to do it. Exercise is also a great stress reliever.

4. **Laugh often.** Laughter is great medicine. In an article by the Mayo Clinic, research shows that the long-term effects of laughter are amazing. Some of the benefits are a stronger immune system, reduced pain levels and better coping skills.

All you really need to do is relax and get out of the way. Your job is to work on controlling your emotions and moods, and staying positive. Listen to your intuition and trust it. God's voice is quiet and still, and may be more of a feeling, or a knowing than anything. The more you walk in faith the better you will get at recognizing it. Start with the small things and work your way up. And journal. Oh, and meditate. Yes. I said it again.

Look Beyond Yourself

"If you're not making someone else's life better, then you're wasting your time. Your life will become better by making other lives better." ~ Will Smith

Another life lesson I have come to know as truth is that we are here to serve others. Once gratitude and forgiveness become part of your being, the natural progression is to start thinking beyond yourself and your own needs. This usually manifests as a desire to help others or positively impact the world in some way. The good thing is that helping others isn't just a nice thing to do it also helps *you*. According to mentalhealth.org, altruism "reduces stress, improves mood, self-esteem, and general happiness." Some research even suggests that helping others can help extend your life (mentalfloss.com).

There are so many ways that I have applied this principle to my own life. My career choice is great example. You see, I have been a financial counselor for over 13 years now and it's still my passion. But I didn't start there. First, I had to get a handle on my own financial situation after the divorce. Once I did, I was moved to help others do the same. That's when I became a counselor. Now, I help my clients figure out a plan to turn around their finances, begin to save, and get out of debt. It's a win-win: my clients get the help they need and I feel good doing it. I love seeing how God gives us beauty for ashes in difficult situations.

Thinking of others doesn't always come naturally, especially in our busy lives. We're all looking down at our phones, rushing to our next appointment, and in our own little worlds. I challenge you today to relax and look up when you walk. Start with small things, such as holding the door for someone or mowing an elderly neighbor's lawn. It really is the simple things that make a difference; I have my own small rituals to remind me of the fact.

One of my favorite things in the world is Tim Horton's coffee. Tim's and I have had a problematic relationship and I had to cut down on consumption. However, once in a while I still treat myself to a cup. When I do, I usually take the opportunity to pay for the car behind me in the drive-through to help bless someone's day. Hopefully, that person will pay it forward to someone else. Another small thing I love to do is give someone my cart at Aldi. The way that is works is you put in a quarter to unlock a cart and get your quarter back when you return it. What I do is pass the cart on if someone is walking up. You see the gesture can be small, but I promise that it *can* change someone's day. We all have the power to uplift others.

Once you start thinking in terms of helping others, opportunities for doing so will naturally begin to appear. They will manifest in all kinds of ways.

A few years ago, my good friend Debi was forced to change careers when she developed carpal tunnel and could no longer work full time on a computer. I introduced her to the Law of Attraction when she was feeling down about leaving her job and starting over. She made a list of the things she needed in a new job, such as having a variety of tasks, so her wrists would get a break, and avoiding the fifty-minute commute that came with her old job. She also wanted a job that made a positive difference in the world. She soon discovered that home healthcare ticked off every box on her wish list. Today, her clients love her (and her cooking, which is phenomenal!).

Debi is happier now than ever before.

Sometimes it seems like the end of the world, but if you trust that there is a plan for you and a reason for what happens in life, misfortune can be a huge blessing.

I realize that not everyone can just up and leave their job to go off and do what they would love to do. Every situation is different.

Several years ago, I had a session with a new client, an attorney. We sat down together to go over her numbers and she was in fine shape: her expenses were less than her income, she could afford to pay all of her bills, and she had a plan to get her student loans paid off. I asked why she had come to see me. She explained that she had never wanted to be a lawyer. She went to law school to please her dad, bought her house because he told her renting was throwing her money away, and was now stuck in this life that made her miserable.

She wanted to be a photographer and travel around the world to help raise awareness about poverty and injustice. She then took out a folded magazine article that described an opportunity to travel to South America to hang out with a famous photographer that was leading the exact life she wanted to lead. I told her that she needed to take that trip and that she should start saving up for it ASAP. She might not be able to leave her job as an attorney right away, but she could take up photography as a hobby and use her vacation time to start following her dreams.

In the meantime, she could do a lot of good as an attorney. She could take on a few pro bono cases a year or raise money for the causes she loved. She walked away from our meeting with the biggest smile on her face because now she had a plan. That is why I love my job.

As a parent, I was proud to discover that, from any early age, my children showed signs of thinking beyond themselves. Now that they are older, I am happy to encourage the development of their generous instincts.

Before Marissa started working, she volunteered to play cards with the residents of a nursing home. She got so much joy out of volunteering, even if she did have to shuffle the deck for each and every person at the table. My daughter was born to work with older people. She loves them and they love her. Thank goodness for people like her because, Lord knows, I do not have the patience for it.

As for Spencer, he has the biggest heart for animals. He has rescued more than one kitten over the years. The first tiny gray kitten he brought home was no more than two or three weeks old and I didn't know if she would make it. She did and we now have her son, Grayson, who is the king of the castle. Our other cat, Tiger was also a Spencer rescue. I picked Spence up from his friend's and we were driving home. He asked me out of the blue how I would feel about another cat, and I told him *not good*. He unzipped his coat and out popped a little guy that was just six or seven weeks old. Spencer said that the kitten's mama had gotten hit and he was homeless. I said "fine". Right now, Tiger is lying next to me, trying to get me to put away the laptop.

It would be great to have a house on a few acres; have a horse or two, some chickens and who knows what else. It would probably turn into a sanctuary of some type.

For my part, I like to give back and there are plenty of causes I could get behind. I would also love to go on a mission trip someday. I sponsored a child through the charity Compassion International for several years until she aged out of the program. I often wonder how she is doing today and if I had an impact in her life. Another one of my passions is safe drinking water. It is unfathomable that this is even an issue in 2019. According to water.org, 1 in 9 people do not have safe drinking water and over 1 million people die every year from diseases linked to contaminated water.

What causes are you passionate about? Animal cruelty, human trafficking, world hunger? Is there something you could do right now where you're at? Could you donate money or time to a local organization in your community? Yes, yes and yes. I encourage you to give back in any way you can.

The point of this life lesson is that everyone can give back in some way. We all have different talents, interests, and passions that we can share and we get to choose how we want to help. Depending on your circumstances, you can donate your time, your skill, your resources, your money, or even all four. You might give back at work, volunteer in your spare time, or collect donations. There are so many ways to give back, I can't possibly list them all here, but, if you want to help, I know you will find a way to help that suits you. I just know that it blesses you to be a blessing to others, and I encourage everyone to do their part.

If you are not sure where to start, here are some suggestions:

1. **Start with your local community.** Help your neighbors, such as mowing lawns, raking leaves, or shopping or cooking for home bound seniors for example. Other ideas include starting a food drive, donating clothing, buying school supplies for needy kids, or adopting a family for the holidays. Have a skill? If you are a hairdresser, you could cut the hair of kids that can't afford it. If you are a handyman, you could do basic home repair for seniors and low-income families. Or, if you can't find any opportunities to help in your community, roll up your sleeves and start one.

2. **Volunteer.** Give your time at a soup kitchen, blood drive or take a turn on your neighborhood watch. Help build with Habitat for Humanity, work at a food drive with your local church, or ring the bell dressed as Santa outside the local Walmart during the holidays. You may

find volunteer opportunities in your area at www.volunteermatch.org.

3. **Support your favorite causes financially.** There are too many to name but make a list of what you would change in the word if you could. We talked about a few earlier and some of the causes I am most passionate about are clean drinking water, animals, ending human trafficking and world hunger. My daughter is an advocate for finding a cure for Alzheimer's and cancer and participates in all of those events. I make monthly donations to K-Love Christian radio, Soi Dog, a dog rescue in the Thailand, and Care for the Needy, an orphanage in Uganda Africa run by one amazing guy. He built their house himself and has documented every step of his organization on Facebook, including planting a garden, harvesting the crops, and distributing every donation of clothing and school supplies he receives. Definitely check him out! I also give to my local church and the local Humane Society chapter, among others.

4. **Just be a kinder person in general.** Hold the door for people that need help and carry heavy items for them, check in on people to see how they are doing. Kindness is contagious and it would be great to be see that spread instead of negativity.

As we come to the end of this lesson, let's go over what you have learned: give back, give back, give back. True fulfillment is all about going beyond yourself and experiencing the joy of giving. It is infectious and I encourage you to begin right now, if you haven't already. Don't forget that you don't have to start a foundation or raise millions to have an impact. In fact, it doesn't have to take a lot of time or money at all. Think about donating just $5 per month to one or more organizations you want to support, or just go help someone right there in your own community. Remember, you will gain as much, if not more, from the experience as the ones you help. Everybody wins when you give.

The Best Is Yet To Come

*"If you can dream it, you can do it." ~**Walt Disney***

Welcome to your final lesson. This is my favorite part of the book, where we get to talk about dreaming and creating the life you want to live. You, my dear, are a co-creator with the Universe- woot, woot! The first time I heard those words I almost cried. When I understood that I had a hand in creating my life, I realized it could be anything I wanted. I don't know about you but I think that's pretty damned exciting!

Just think about it: you don't have to stay in a dead end job that you hate; you don't have to stay stuck in that toxic relationship; you don't have to stay stuck in a place you don't like; and you don't have to stay broke. Instead, you can find that ideal career; you can have a healthy relationship; you can live where you want; and you can turn around your finances. You can change any aspect of your life and choose to create a better future for yourself.

So far, we've looked at each lesson separately, but it's time now to pull everything together and learn how you can create a new framework for your life. Each step in the sequence contains the next activity or two you may use in creating your best life.

If you haven't already, go ahead and take that first step right now, so you can start living the life you desire today.

1. **Get clear on what you want.** Yes, we are going to journal again. Get used to it, my dear. You might have noticed I talked a lot about writing down your dreams and goals throughout this book. It is so necessary in activating the Law of Attraction into your life. The Universe loves clarity. Make a list and get detailed about what your ideal life would look like. Focus on the five senses- smell, touch, taste, sight and sound, and go into as much detail as possible. If a new car is your goal describe the new car smell, the feel of the leather, the sound of the stereo and revving engine for example.

   Address any negative feelings and *fears* that come up. Fears try to keep you small and inside your comfort zone. In order to have all that is meant for you, conquering your fears is necessary. That little voice will tell you things like you can't do that, you're not smart enough, pretty enough blah blah blah. It's time to get rid of all the negative and fear-based self-talk once and for all. On a separate piece of paper write down those thoughts or feelings to get them out but then destroy that paper. You can rip it up, shred it or even burn it. Remember- keep positive journal entries, destroy negative ones.

2. **Raise your vibrational energy.** Remember that like attracts like so you need to keep your thoughts positive as much as possible. That doesn't mean you will never have a bad day or feel upset. Allow yourself to fully feel your emotions but then work to quickly shift your mood. Take some advice from Taylor Swift and "Shake it off".

You can raise your vibe by listening to music, dancing, going for a walk, exercising, meditating, listening to a motivational speaker like Tony Robbins or Oprah, watching a funny video, basically anything that lights you up. Get purposeful with this, and keep doing it until it becomes like second nature. The goal is to be happy and content the majority of the time.

3. **Work on healing your past.** In order to manifest your dreams, you have to let go of anything that is holding you back. Your childhood issues, anger, wounds from relationships, or whatever you are holding onto needs to be healed in order to live life to the fullest. You can talk to a therapist; you can use personal development. There are many ways to approach healing. What worked best for me was journal dumping and meditation. Journal dumping is where you write down anything and everything that comes to mind. You get everything out on paper and then destroy it when you're done. Nobody else is going to read it. Release all the shame and guilt and most private thoughts and fears. Do this as many times as you need to. Whenever you get triggered, do it again. I did this over a two-ear period before I finally felt free.

4. **Create positive affirmations and mantras.** Once you start working on that negative mindset and you get all of those limiting beliefs out of your head, you'll want to replace them with positive, life-affirming thoughts. Create a list of positive phrases to feed to your subconscious. Phrases such as: I am amazing, I am

generous, I am smart, I am good with money. Take limiting beliefs and problem areas and state their opposite in the most positive, self-affirming way possible. Repeat these affirmations anytime you feel the need for a boost. Try saying them to yourself out loud in front of the bathroom mirror until you believe them.

5. **Get rid of clutter and create some space.** Now that you know what you want and have started replacing limiting beliefs with positive ones, it's time to start making room for what you want in the physical world. Declutter closets, organize drawers, clean out your purse and wallets. What I am talking about here is physically cleaning up and getting rid of junk, clutter, and mess in all areas of your life. This lets the Universe know that you are serious! If you want more money, make room in your wallet. If you want a partner, clear out part of your closet so there would be room for their clothing. If you want new furniture get the room ready by painting and sprucing it up. It may sound silly but creating physical space in your life makes room for new things, people, and experiences to come into your life.

6. **Create a vision board.** This last step is about keeping you emotionally connected to your desired outcome; it is one of my favorite activities. It is about creating a visual representation of your dreams. You can do this the old-fashioned way, using a physical poster board, or, you can use digital tools, such as an online platform like Pinterest, image editing software, or even your favorite word processing application. You can Google images

and either print and paste them on the board or paste them in virtual space. If you create your vision board on your computer, I would still recommend printing it out so you can display it somewhere.

A creative alternative to traditional vision boarding is surrounding yourself with relevant images by taping them to your walls. For example, if you are calling in more money, put up monopoly money all over your walls. One of my favorite stories in *The Secret* is the one about Jack Canfield writing $100,000 on a dollar bill and taping it to his ceiling so it would be the first thing he saw every morning when he woke up. ,

Those are the main action steps that I used to beat a ten-year period of severe depression. I tried going down the traditional therapy and anti-depressant route but it just didn't help. The Law of Attraction (aka LOA), on the other hand, did work. It really made sense to me, and once I began applying its principles, I realized I had found the missing piece of the puzzle; this was what I had been looking for all along.

Here are some final tips for super-charging the Law of Attraction and creating the life you desire:

1. **Stop saying: "don't," "can't," "I'm not"**. Watch how you speak. Your words create your reality. Stop saying: "I can't afford that," "I'm not good at this," "I don't know how to do that," and so forth. Instead, flip the switch and say: "I am worthy," "I am successful," "I am prosperous." Instead of saying, "I can't afford it," say, "It's not in the

budget right now." This one can be difficult because our words are ingrained in us, they come from childhood and beyond and run deep. Keep working at this one as it may take some time.

2. **Act as if you already have what you desire.** This doesn't mean you should write checks when the money is not in the bank. What I'm talking about here is a mindset thing. Act as if what you want is on its way. Talk about the future, and how you want things to be. As with the decluttering stage, you are making room in your life for the things you are calling in. For example, if you are dreaming of having a new house, you could take advantage of a sale to pick up the kitchen supplies and household goods you're going to need in the future.

3. **Let go of resistance.** Stop worrying and being anxious about the "how" and "when". In fact, stop thinking about them all together. Go about your life. Act as if what you want is coming but do not stress over when or how it will come. Your job is to focus on your mindset and emotions, not to sweat the details.

4. **Surround yourself with like-minded people.** In order to stay in a positive frame of mind, you need to surround yourself with people who are uplifting, happy, and see the world through rose colored glasses. Find yourself a tribe that knows the glass is half full and that lifts you up. I belong to several Facebook Law of Attraction groups, watch videos on manifesting, read personal development books, and listen to podcasts. I *never* watch

the news, scary or violent movies, and I avoid people who bring me down. As you become more positive, there will be people that drop out of your life. This can be painful because they may even be family members or long-time friends. You can't do much about that, if you want to move forward. Just know that the people who are meant to be there will remain.

5. **Forgive those you are angry with.** I know this one is difficult but it is a must. Make a list of anyone you are struggling to forgive and get to work on this beast of a task. Write a letter of forgiveness to each and every person on your list. Don't worry about what you say because you will destroy it when you are finished. Sincerity is key so keep at it. It will get easier. You may have to do this a few times for some people on your list. Cord cutting journeys or childhood healing meditations are also great forgiveness techniques. Search for some on You Tube and give it a try.

6. **Be grateful.** Start saying thank you to God, the Universe, or Source (pick your term) for all things small and large in your life. Be thankful for what you already have, so more can come in. Appreciate all the good people in your life, from your family members to the waitress at the local diner. Say thank you for scoring a great parking spot, or finding a quarter on the ground. Be grateful for a refund that comes in the mail or a gift card you receive. Start a gratitude journal and make daily entries. Gratitude is huge and will unlock more blessings to come into your life.

7. **Meditate.** If you didn't think I would mention this at least one more time you were wrong. Make mediation a part of your daily routine for the rest of your life.

8. **Keep going.** Never give up. Life will most certainly give you lessons but you are strong. If you get knocked down, get up again. Dust yourself, my dear, and keep going.

I love you all,

Beth

Conclusion

"A Champion is defined not by their wins but how they can recover when they fall" ~ **Serena Williams**

We have reached the end of this book but it is just the beginning of your journey. You now have a blueprint to get your life on track and moving again. If you go through the life lessons and do the work, I know you can create the life you want, whether you are twenty-five or seventy-five. Don't worry, you still have time to figure it out, because, well, you're still breathing.

Before I let you go, I want to leave you with some final thoughts and words of encouragement.

I wrote this book is to let you know that it's completely okay if you are not where you thought you would be in life right now. Maybe it's just that you still don't know what you want to be when you grow up. That's such a silly phrase, honestly, because we all just keep growing and evolving throughout our lifetimes. I certainly never imagined I would become an author or that I would have a message to share.

My first parting words are, drop the guilt and work on self-love. If you don't accept who you are, if you don't get over the guilt, you will have a really hard time moving forward, your self-development will stall. If you struggle with self-acceptance, pay extra attention to life lesson #4, because, until you come to terms with yourself, the changes just won't stick.

The other piece of advice I want to share with you is that dreaming is not only okay, it's your next assignment. Take some time to write out what you want your life to look like and don't be afraid to get down to the details. Use journaling, vision boarding, mediation, and all of the other practices I recommend in this book, to go from dreaming to active co-creation. It's time to manifest your best life!

I am so excited for you, my dear! I know that great things are already happening for you as you read these words.

Finally, I want to let you know that I am interested in your journey and that I have created a special place for us to connect. If you would like to share your story, talk about your dreams, and meet similarly minded people, just search Facebook groups for "Dust Yourself Off My Dear" and join our wonderful, positive-only community. Can't wait to hear from you!

Best wishes,

Beth

Photos of Marissa, Spencer and I

About the Author

Beth Blanco is an author, speaker, financial counselor, and Mindset Coach with a passion for helping others live their best financial and personal lives.

Beth began doing financial counseling in 2005 and received her Accredited Financial Counselor (AFC®) certification from AFCPE®. She spent six years as a budget counselor at the University of Michigan Credit Union and another four and a half years at Habitat for Humanity doing financial counseling for their clientelle, and many years self-employed as well. Beth also holds a B.A. in business from Siena Heights University in Adrian, MI. Her first book, *Get Your Sh*t Together with Your Money*, is now available on Amazon.

Beth began her mindset work in 2016, after experiencing the transformative power of the Law of Attraction. She lives in Michigan with her son Spencer.

Connect with Beth:
Facebook group: Money Minds
www.moneymindsonline.com
beth@moneymindsonline.com